WHAT'S MY DOG THINKING?

UNDERSTAND
YOUR DOG TO GIVE
THEM A HAPPY LIFE

HANNAH MOLLOY

DK Penguin Random House

Project Editor Andrea Page
Project Art Editor Alison Gardner
Senior Editor Alastair Laing
Editorial Assistant Kiron Gill
US Editor Kayla Dugger
Senior Designer Saffron Stocker
Managing Editor Dawn Henderson
Managing Art Editor Marianne Markham
Senior Production Editor Tony Phipps
Production Controller Rebecca Parton
Jacket Designer Saffron Stocker
Jacket Co-ordinator Lucy Philpott
Art Director Maxine Pedliham
Publishing Director Mary-Clare Jerram

Illustrations Mark Scheibmayr

First American Edition, 2020
Published in the United States by DK Publishing
1450 Broadway, Suite 801, New York, NY 10018

Text copyright © Hannah Molloy, 2020
Copyright © 2020 Dorling Kindersley Limited
DK, a Division of Penguin Random House LLC
21 22 23 24 10 9 8 7 6 5 4 3
009–318362–Nov/2020

Hannah Molloy has asserted her right to be
identified as the author of this work.

Published in Great Britain
by Dorling Kindersley Limited

A catalog record for this book
is available from the Library of Congress.

ISBN 978-1-4654-9942-4

Printed and bound in China

For the curious

www.dk.com

MIX
Paper from
responsible sources
FSC™ C018179

Contents

Foreword

I'm a dog geek, for life. As a baby, I was bitten on the face by a rescue dog and sat in shock but never cried. It's a family joke that I've had dog in my blood ever since, because I've never found them anything short of fascinating. I opened my first pet sitting business at 9 years old, and at 12, earned the right to have my first dog—a Cavalier King Charles Spaniel called Beano.

I have studied and worked professionally with dogs for more than 15 years, and I've trained more than 10,000 dogs—and just as many owners. Since earning an Honors Degree in Animal Behavior and becoming a fully qualified dog behaviorist, my focus has been on dog language and culture: what we know, what we think we know, and what we don't know. Once I realized that dogs can smell cancer, my love for them went supernova. But I also saw that even though these incredible animals could smell disease, humans were still smacking their noses as discipline, holding them by the throat until they submitted and pushing their butts into the ground rather than asking them to sit. Dogs are sensitive and easy to train, if we just take the time to watch and understand them.

Once you start interpreting dog body language, it's a skill you never turn off. After reading this book, you'll start noticing dog "chats" every day. I want to help people step into the world of the canine "detective." I hope this book will give you the eye and the insight to dogwatch as a fascinating hobby—and to look at, love, and learn from your dog in a brand new way. What we thought we knew about dog behavior 20 years ago has changed so much, and one day we'll know even more. While this book is an up-to-date compendium of postures agreed upon by the world's best dog geeks, I for one will never stop asking, "What's my dog thinking?"

Start to think like a dog

In order to start working out what your dog is thinking, it's important to understand how dogs think—in particular, the way they communicate and experience the world, and the key instincts and processes driving their behavior.

How dogs communicate

Dogs constantly talk to us, and each other, with posture and movement and through sounds and scent—whether we notice it or not! To become a dog detective and understand how your dog thinks, first identify the clues from their postures and sounds, and discover the depth of their world of smell.

Communicating with posture

We dog body language geeks are always analyzing how a dog stands; what the tail is doing; how the eyes, ears, and mouth look; and lots more. Each part of the body is like a letter in the dog's body language; together, they form a posture, or "word," that's a snapshot of what the dog is saying in that moment. A fluid, moving sequence of postures gives us the dog's full "sentence." This book is full of postures that are analyzed to help you learn to read your dog—while the "Advanced dogwatching" features will help you master more complex full sentences of behavior. It's really important to start by simply observing parts of your dog's body without trying to analyze them right away. Each is one piece of the bigger story.

Body

Are the body and stance relaxed and loose, or is there muscle tension and stiffness? Is the dog's posture tall or lowered? Is their weight placed forward, backward, or is it neutral? Bunched fur can also reveal physical and emotional tension. Try to avoid assumptions; for example, a dog that has rolled over could be either friendly or frightened (see pages 32–33).

Ears

Ear position can tell you which direction the dog is thinking about. Forward ears are alert to what's ahead; pulled-back ears may mean the dog wants to move backward. If one ear is forward and one back, the dog is listening to two sources of sound and may be making a decision, while "airplane" ears going out to the side are a sign the dog is guarding their personal space or an item.

Face

Can you see the dog's facial muscles, and are they tense or relaxed? Is the brow held in a tension frown?

Eyes

Look at the eyes: are they "hard" and bulbous, or "soft" and almond shaped? Are they blinking or staring? Are the pupils dilated (big) or constricted (small)? Can you see the whites of the eyes? What are the eyes focusing on?

Mouth

Is the dog's mouth open and panting, or is it closed? How far out is the tongue, and is it "spatulate" (wider at the bottom)? Can you see pronounced teeth? If the dog is showing you their teeth by curling a lip or panting with lips pulled back, there's a reason—they are probably warning you to give them some space.

Tail

Wagging doesn't always mean happy. The tail has several functions for dogs, including communication; if it's tucked between the legs or the dog is sitting down, it can signal anxiety. Note the height, tension, and speed of the dog's tail moment to moment. For more on reading the tail, turn to pages 18–19.

See the whole dog
Whatever your dog's unique features, be sure to look at their body language as a whole—from nose to tail.

Continued »

Communicating with scent

Dogs experience the world very differently to humans because their primary sense is smell—they smell before they see. And it's incredibly powerful; relative to overall brain size, the area in a dog's brain dealing with olfaction (smell) is 40 times larger than ours, and dogs may have as many as 300 million nasal scent receptors, compared to our 6 million—they can detect a teaspoon of sugar in enough water to fill two Olympic swimming pools! The sides of dogs' nostrils let air (and scent) circulate constantly, and they sniff separately through each nostril, helping them triangulate and locate where an odor came from.

Pheromones

A huge part of dog communication happens through their ability to detect and analyze pheromones: chemical signals that prompt a social reaction in the same species. Pheromones are

Detecting and secreting pheromones

The vomeronasal organ (VNO) detects pheromones in scent particles; the dog may flare nostrils, curl a top lip, or "chatter" teeth to gather these. The tongue flicks particles into the incisive papilla, to the VNO. Nerves in the VNO send electrical signals directly to the secondary olfactory bulb, which relays signals to areas of the brain that trigger behavioral/emotional responses.

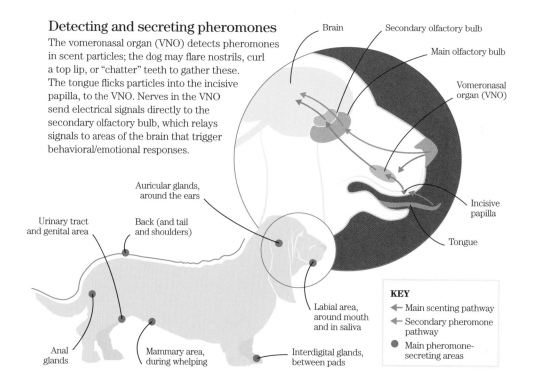

Brain

Secondary olfactory bulb

Main olfactory bulb

Vomeronasal organ (VNO)

Incisive papilla

Tongue

Auricular glands, around the ears

Urinary tract and genital area

Back (and tail and shoulders)

Anal glands

Mammary area, during whelping

Interdigital glands, between pads

Labial area, around mouth and in saliva

KEY
← Main scenting pathway
← Secondary pheromone pathway
● Main pheromone-secreting areas

secreted from scent glands all over the dog's body and reveal their age, sex, reproductive status, health, emotional state, and more. Dogs sniff each other to gain all this valuable information and have a secondary olfactory system for processing pheromones via a vomeronasal organ (VNO) in the roof of the mouth. They also wag their tails to waft scent messages. This amazing sensory ability also allows dogs to communicate remotely—their waste broadcasts what they've eaten, their mood, how long since they were there, and even the direction they were going in. If your dog sniffs and licks, they may be scenting prey or putting urine on their VNO for analysis; when they stop to pee, they're engaging in their own vital form of social media.

Communicating with sounds

Dogs vocalize anything from questions to concerns, appeals, warnings, and friendly hellos. Asking the following questions can help you work out what your dog is saying:

What's the context?
What's going on around the dog just before and after they make the sound? What does that tell you about what they want it to achieve?

What's the pitch?
- **High pitch**: These sounds are designed to attract your attention.
- **Low pitch**: Warning vocalizations are often guttural and low.
- **Alternating pitch**: High to low to high again is used as "chatter" to appease and to ask you for things.

What kind of sound?
- **One bark** is the classic alert—or "What's that?"—bark.
- **Several barks**: The more barks there are, the more urgent it is for your dog—even if it's just a ball that's stuck under the couch.
- **Growling bark**: This can be a frustrated alert bark or, depending on body language, a play invitation.
- **Squealing** can signal fear, joy, or surprise.
- **Whining** is a pleading sound: your dog wants something.
- **Howling** is a cry for social contact or an attempt to build a social bond through "singing."
- **"Ruff," "huff," "bow," or "woo"**: The sound of each dog's verbal language varies, depending on the shape of their mouth.

Dog breeds

Dogs have walked alongside us for millennia, although most modern breeds were actually shaped during the last two centuries. Today, there are over 350 pedigree breeds, plus countless marvelous mixed and crossbreeds! It's important to understand that a dog's breed can impact the way they think, behave, and use body language to communicate.

What is your dog's breed group?

Every single dog has a breed group somewhere in their DNA. Over many thousands of years, humans bred dogs for particular functions, like guarding our homes, finding and chasing our food, and dispatching vermin. As our needs changed, these roles shifted and looks also became far more important. But a dog's basic genetic "job" still matters—dogs will do what their breed group traits tell them when they are excited or stressed. Unless we satisfy breed-based drives in training and everyday life, our dogs' behavior is also likely to confuse or annoy us, and we can easily mislabel it (see pages 24–25). While different countries have their own breed classifications, they all fit into one of the seven broad trait groups shown opposite.

Bred to bring stuff
Many Gundogs were bred to find and fetch game or birds and love retrieving … even in water.

Breed groups

Herding dogs

Herding dogs are super-smart team players that learn human cues fast. They need 2 hours of problem solving every day—even if it's just managing a ball—and they can struggle in busy social situations without something to focus on.

Popular breeds include: Australian Shepherd, Belgian Shepherd, Border Collie, Shetland Sheepdog

Spitz types

Spitz types are socially intelligent, mentally and physically strong, and enjoy a mixture of hunting, guarding, and pulling. With their wolflike independence, this group won't take you seriously if you baby them.

Popular breeds include: Akita, Alaskan Malamute, Shiba Inu, Siberian Husky

Terriers

Terriers are sassy, quick, smart, intense, often noisy, and bite and chase things that run. They usually throw themselves at problems and have the lowest frustration tolerance of any breed group.

Popular breeds include: Airedale Terrier, Border Terrier, Cairn Terrier, Jack Russell Terrier, Staffordshire Bull Terrier

Gundogs

Gundogs are clever, praise-seeking, and love to be busy at work, finding and fetching things. Whether a Gundog breed naturally prefers water, woods, or long grass, their energy is typically boundless!

Popular breeds include: English Springer Spaniel, German Shorthaired Pointer, Golden Retriever, Hungarian Vizsla, Labrador Retriever, Weimeraner

Guarding dogs

Guarding dogs are intelligent, independent problem solvers who want to control their environment, making them loyal; fearlessly brave; and, as adults, naturally suspicious of anything new. Some breeds in this group need high levels of mental and physical exercise daily.

Popular breeds include: Dobermann, German Shepherd (also has Herding traits), Mastiff, Rottweiler

Hounds

Hounds are hunters by sight or smell, often bred to work in groups. They need to use their amazing skills to discover treasure, and they will … with or without you!

Popular breeds include: Beagle, Basset Hound, Greyhound, Saluki, Whippet

Toy dogs

These guys are often mini-versions of another breed type, and with similar traits, although half-size doesn't necessarily mean half the work! However, certain Toy breeds were bred as companions or lapdogs and enjoy human contact and attention.

Popular breeds include: Chihuahua, French Bulldog, Italian Greyhound, Papillon, Pomeranian, Pug, Toy Poodle

Continued ≫

Breed adaptations

The fashion for owning pedigree breeds, and the resulting focus on obtaining "ideal" breed features, has led to physical issues for some breeds, ranging from pronounced skin folds to higher rates of deafness. These, and other adaptations that humans have imposed on dogs, can sometimes act as a barrier to communication. If your dog has features like those listed here, be aware when they are socializing with other dogs, and especially with children. "Calming signals" that dogs naturally offer to keep things relaxed may not be as clear coming from these dogs, and they will get frustrated if they don't feel heard. All dog play bouts need good communication, and a lack of this may potentially lead to tension or aggression.

No tail

Tails tell us so much about how dogs are feeling, from a gentle, friendly wag to hiding the anal glands in anxiety (see pages 18–19). Breeds without full tails include Boston Terriers, Brittany Spaniels, and French Bulldogs.

Brachycephalic breeds

Breeds such as Bulldogs, Boxers, Mastiffs, and Pugs have shortened snouts, so they can't breathe well or flex as many facial muscles as other breeds. They often have to use exaggerated body wiggles to appease other dogs and invite play; this can come across as too intense, sometimes leading to social exclusion.

Flattened face

The facial features of bull breeds like English Bull Terriers and Staffordshire Bull Terriers can make these dogs look strange to other dogs, affecting their ability to make friends.

Black-coated dogs

These dogs' facial expressions can be more difficult for other dogs and people to discern and read, which means they often get overlooked at rescue centers.

Docking and pinning

Docking helps prevent life-threatening damage to the tails of specified working breeds. However, pinning— chopping off part of the ear—is done to prevent a dog being able to appease with their body and to make them more intimidating to other dogs, thereby increasing the risk of aggressive encounters.

Breeding trends

Crossbreeds are a mix of two pedigree or pure breeds, whereas the parentage of a mixed-breed dog may include more or is unknown. While overall these dogs are healthier than pedigrees, the rebranding of many crossbreeds—especially Poodle mixes—into "designer dogs" has led to soaring price tags, even though the breeders aren't regulated. A registered pedigree provides a family tree of health-tested dogs and holds the breeder accountable if the puppy has health or behavioral problems. When you buy a puppy from a breeder, use this checklist to make sure they can prove the pup is healthy and set up to succeed socially.

Buyer's checklist:

- [ ] **The pups are all together** and with their mom in the breeder's home (not a barn or cage), and are flea free and clean smelling.
- [ ] **The mom is confident** and calm with you and doesn't bark when you come to the door.
- [ ] **The pups are fed** in separate bowls, have access to toys, and have clearly separated sleeping and pottying areas.
- [ ] **The breeder has proof** of health tests for both parents, including for any genetic disorders associated with the breeds involved.
- [ ] **The pups are 8–12 weeks old**. This is the most trainable age, which should be reflected in the price.
- [ ] **The breeder can show** you a socialization chart that tracks each pup's interaction with household sights and noises, people, animals, travel, and handling.
- [ ] **The pups are pretrained** and are able to potty away from their beds, be separated from each other for short periods, be handled, and sit.

Look beyond the color

As black dogs' facial details are harder to see, understanding their body language is even more important.

17

The art of dogwatching

Now you know more about the detailed body language dogs use to tell us how they're feeling, and how breeding can affect this, it's time to start observing your dog. Here are some top tips on the practice of dogwatching and the importance of seeing dogs' behavior in its full context.

How to start dogwatching

Take off your glasses

We all have a pair of "perspective glasses" that color our thinking; you might wear a pair of "Labradors forever" glasses, "My dog's nervous around other dogs" glasses, or "I'm the top dog" glasses. To really learn about dogs, you have to observe the measurable facts first before trying to interpret a situation. For example, if another dog faces yours at the park and paws at the ground:

- **Glasses on**: "That dog's asserting dominance over my dog."
- **Glasses off**: "That dog smelled my dog's bottom, walked away, urinated on a tree, faced my dog, then scratched the ground with all four feet for three seconds."

Film your dog

Dogs see the world a split second quicker than us. Even when we're watching them closely, things can happen so fast, we may miss some subtleties of dog "chats." To build your dogwatching skills, film your dog's interactions and watch them in stop-start to spot key signals that you will have missed in real time.

Keep calm ... and smile

We can't always watch our dogs like scientists from a distance; we are often "in" the situations ourselves, and as such we will have an effect on them, too. It's easy to find ourselves scolding our dogs if we're not sure what they're up to, or they're messing around. But tension in the voice or yanking on the lead create more problems, whereas being cheerful—even when we don't feel fully in control—can make a situation less tense. So chill out!

Trust yourself

That said, sometimes you have to act to keep yourself, other people, or your dog safe in the moment. Trust your gut instinct and go with it.

Dogwatching focus: the tail

Assuming that a wagging tail equals a happy dog is like assuming someone is friendly because they're waving without looking at what their hand is doing. Let's look objectively at what a dog's tail position and speed may actually be telling you.

What's the tail for?

Tails are limbs designed to help dogs balance and communicate. They provide a visual signal in long grass and control how much of a dog's signature scent information is wagged at the world. Dogs can spread their signature by wagging, or disguise it by tucking their tail between their legs or sitting down to cover the anal glands. So a dog's tail offers valuable information on their mood.

Is position important?

- **Yes: a high tail** tells us the dog has had an adrenaline rush and is aroused, which can mean they're either excited or scared; both have the same effect on the body.
- **A low tail** suggests the dog feels nervous or anxious, because they may be about to cover their anal glands in order to "hide" in their world of smell, as we might hide behind sunglasses. But it can be friendly, too. Dogs often drop their tail when focusing on something, like an interesting smell.

What about speed?

- **A fast-moving tail** can mean the dog is either anxious or excited.
- **A high, quivering tail** is often a sign the dog is about to chase something or have a potentially moody encounter with another dog.

So what is a "happy" tail?

A low, gently sweeping wag is a nice, friendly gesture, but the true helicopter "tail of joy" goes up, down, and around in circles—usually when you arrive home! Keep watching your dog's tail in different situations, but don't focus on it entirely; it's only one part of the whole picture.

Tail of happiness
A fast wag as your dog jumps up at you shows joyful excitement.

Continued »

Seeing the bigger picture

In this book, you'll find lots of freeze-frame postures that dogs use to tell us how they're feeling in any given moment. Watching out for as many of these as possible in real life will help you gain a deeper understanding of your dog. But being the best possible dog detective means being aware of what's going on around your dog, too.

Zooming in

As you learn more about dog body language, it is easy to focus too much on one part of the body or a specific behavior. But to really understand dogs, it's important to step back and look at the wider context. For example, what if a dog pees on the couch? If we zoom in on the dog, we

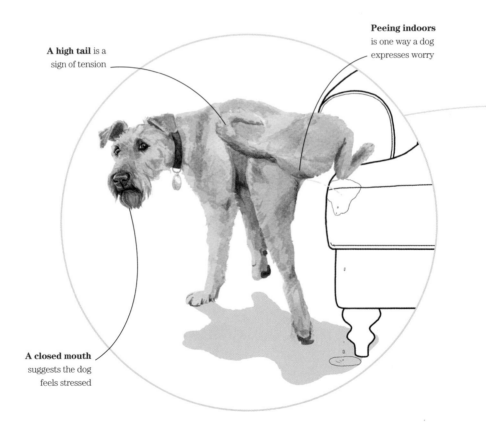

A high tail is a sign of tension

Peeing indoors is one way a dog expresses worry

A closed mouth suggests the dog feels stressed

could easily label this as "bad" because peeing on furniture is not okay. But focusing on the behavior alone may lead to using a punishment like a spray collar to "fix" it and stop the dog marking indoors.

Zooming out

Dogs often store up the emotions and stresses of the household and reflect them back in their behavior. So by zooming out, we suddenly see that children play fighting nearby may be loud and scary for the dog, the cat may have hit the dog on the nose for getting too close, and a drink has been knocked over in the excitement. As an experienced behaviorist, these all tell me that, actually, the dog is stressed out. Rather than punishing the dog, I would stop the wrestling match, clean up the drink, and teach my cat better manners! Spooked dogs often stress-pee because it helps calm them down. Read on to find out why it's so important to also consider the *function* of any behavior for your dog (see pages 22–23).

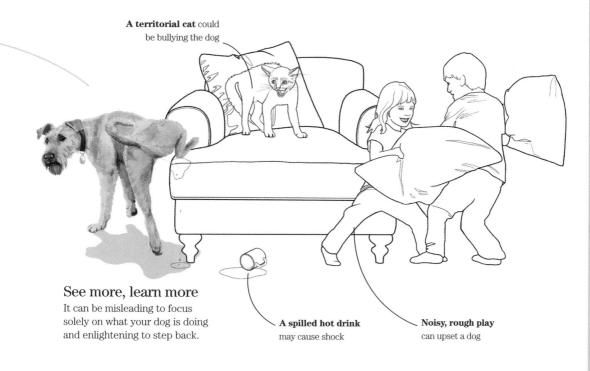

A territorial cat could be bullying the dog

See more, learn more

It can be misleading to focus solely on what your dog is doing and enlightening to step back.

A spilled hot drink may cause shock

Noisy, rough play can upset a dog

What's the function?

Your dog's behavior isn't good or bad—it just is. But if you're confused, worried, or just amused by what they're doing, you can turn dog detective and find out what's really going on by asking one key question: "What's the function for my dog?"

It's easy to put human explanations and comedy subtitles over our dogs' weirder habits and expressions; now we'll consider the actual function. This is key to understanding our dogs, because they don't think of their choices as right or wrong—they ask, "Is this useful for my survival, or not?" If you don't know why your dog is doing something, apply the "What's the function?" formula to work out what they want to achieve in that situation. Examine what you or another person or animal did before the behavior, the environment around your dog, what happened afterward, and their specific body language. Once you have done this, identifying the type of behavior (see opposite) will also help you decide how to respond. Many of the behaviors shown in this book apply this strategy to understand what dogs are thinking—look out for clues to the function.

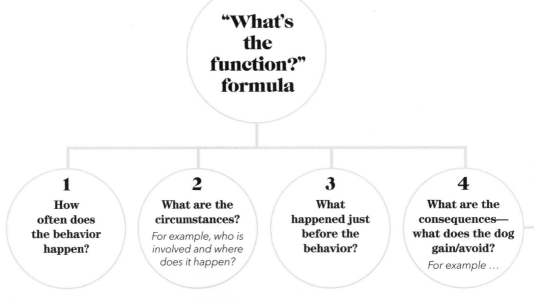

"What's the function?" formula

1
How often does the behavior happen?

2
What are the circumstances?
For example, who is involved and where does it happen?

3
What happened just before the behavior?

4
What are the consequences—what does the dog gain/avoid?
For example …

... does the dog gain:

- Attention or company?
- Access to something they like?
- Relaxation or relief?
- Nutrition?
- A toy or treat?
- A sense of achievement?

... does the dog avoid:

- Confrontation or attack?
- Pain or fear?
- Frustration?
- Losing something, like a toy?

Behavior types

Understanding which category your dog's behavior falls into will help you work out what the dog is thinking and what you should do:

- **Calming signals**, such as lip licking and yawning, help dogs reduce tension, express fear, or avoid arguments in social situations. Spotting them and responding quickly stops things escalating toward aggression.
- **Learned behaviors** are reinforced when they pay off for your dog and reduced when they don't. These are conscious decisions your dog makes, but they can be unlearned. Some behaviors are both learned and conditioned (see below). For example, your dog could have a conditioned fear response on seeing nail clippers and then show aggression, which they have learned can make grooming stop.
- **Classically conditioned behaviors** happen without thinking and are linked to an emotional or physical response. If you always yank the lead when your dog meets another dog, your dog will become conditioned to feeling fear, as this is repeatedly associated with being strangled and frustrated whenever they see another dog.
- **Ritualized behaviors** are softened or exaggerated versions of key survival skills, adapted over time for social use, such as growling and snapping the air during an altercation, rather than actual biting or noisy play fighting.
- **Displacement behaviors** like scratching or excessive drinking are ordinary but oddly timed behaviors that usually signal social discomfort or stress, like looking at your phone in a busy elevator.
- **Atavistic behaviors** are no longer needed for survival but still occur, like dogs circling before lying down on their mat to flatten invisible grass.
- **Sexual behaviors** are, well ... you know!
- **Predatory behaviors** help a dog find and kill things to eat.
- **Maladaptive behaviors** feel good in the short term but are harmful to survival in the long term, like dogs chasing their tail or us eating junk food.

Mislabeling behaviors

Labels are sticky and hard to remove, so let's not apply them to our dogs. The only label your dog really needs ... is "dog."

We know that for dogs, there's no such thing as "good" or "bad" behavior; they only do what's useful for their survival in the moment. That is why labeling your dog as stupid or difficult—or even "princess," "top dog," or "a rescue"—is a fundamental mistake. It will affect your view of everything your dog does *and* your response, so it will always be impossible for them to exceed your expectations. These are a few of the labels often attached to dogs.

"Stubborn"

It can seem like a dog knows what you want and is intentionally not doing it. More often than not, they either have no idea what you want them to do and are sitting still, hoping you'll explain or go away, and/or you're not using the right reward to motivate them.

"Guilty"

Right and wrong are human concepts, so if your dog ate your sandwich while you left the room, it's because it was a useful decision in that moment; they don't even remember it by the time you get back! We only think dogs know they've done something wrong and feel guilty because they're so good

at reading our faces and avoiding arguments; when you come back in scowling, they offer behaviors to appease you, like lip licking and rolling over. Ignoring these calming signals will teach dogs to bite (pages 150–151).

"Dominant"

The dominance myth has colored the glasses we use to view dogs for too long. Like any social species, dogs want to show each other who's the fastest, tallest, and strongest, as these are key survival skills. But they don't assert dominance over each other as a natural behavior; even wolves live in family units rather than hierarchical packs. Nor is a dog trying to get one over on you by walking ahead, peeing in the house, or growling at you over food. Assuming they are means we'll treat them more harshly and ruin their capacity to trust us in the name of "respect." You really don't need to be the alpha—we already choose when our dogs eat, where they walk, and their friendships. Rolling a dog over to submit to you is basically bullying. Most will cope with it, but some insecure dogs will learn to bully back or even bite—all because of a label.

Trigger stacking

Dogs labeled as unpredictable, unfriendly, or aggressive may actually have freaked out due to "trigger stacking." While a single event may cause them some stress, if these triggers happen in a sequence, it can eventually tip the dog over a threshold—and they may suddenly bark and lunge, shut down, or hide.

We've all experienced the straw that breaks the camel's back. On a good day, our stress levels are low and we feel okay, but on another day, if we spill coffee, mislay keys, then get stuck in traffic, it can build up to us exploding with rage at another driver or co-worker. It's the same for dogs; their triggers are anything that causes excitement, worry, discomfort, or frustration. Each event winds them up a little more, until all it takes is one final straw—even just a dog barking at them—to send them over their stress threshold so that they burst into "unpredictable" aggression, freeze, or even run away. They can't access calm behavior again without our help.

Managing a triggered dog:

- **Your dog** is having a panic attack and can't hear you. Help them escape the situation and give them time and space to calm down.
- **Don't shout at or check** your dog if they're barking or lunging, for

How stacking works
Each event raises the dog's tension level, often without you noticing, until they snap.

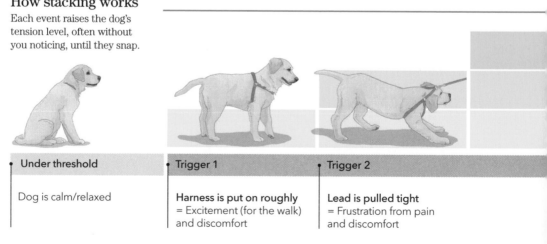

Under threshold	Trigger 1	Trigger 2
Dog is calm/relaxed	**Harness is put on roughly** = Excitement (for the walk) and discomfort	**Lead is pulled tight** = Frustration from pain and discomfort

instance, by yanking on the lead—they'll learn to see you as one more "monster" in an already scary situation. While it might stop the barking in the moment, it won't change the underlying emotion and could make their reactions even more unpredictable in future.

Preventing trigger stacking:

- **Study your dog's body language** so you can spot subtle signs of rising tension. Wait for the dog to literally shake off the effects of one trigger, by shaking their whole body, before letting them encounter the next scary or exciting thing.

- **Learn to recognize** your dog's triggers, then treat each one as a separate training goal to teach the dog that triggers can also mean fun.

For example, if your dog is reactive toward other dogs, use treats to teach your dog to look at and then look away from other dogs from a distance, where your dog can be relaxed, then move in closer. Try a "relaxation week" of training sessions instead of walks, if your dog gets highly stressed outdoors.

- **Loose-lead walking** and long-line training reduce physical tension while your dog is on the lead, helping them feel relaxed, while treat training can help change frustration or fear to positive anticipation (see pages 170–171).

- **Encourage your dog** to do some sniffing while they're under their threshold, and praise relaxed posture. Your dog's good day is your good day, too!

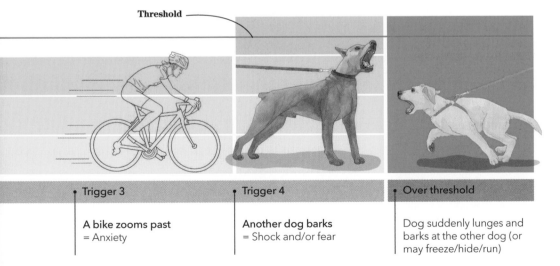

Threshold

Trigger 3

A bike zooms past
= Anxiety

Trigger 4

Another dog barks
= Shock and/or fear

Over threshold

Dog suddenly lunges and barks at the other dog (or may freeze/hide/run)

CHAPTER ONE

My amazing dog

Our talented dogs have a multitude of ways to express themselves. In this chapter, discover some of the wonderful—and often weird—body language that dogs use to tell us exactly how they're feeling.

My dog is always licking his nose

Why does my dog lick his nose and lips so often? It's like "Tongue Out Tuesday" every day—and he'll regularly do a major nose wipe with his gymnastic tongue!

the function?

Nose and lip licking tells people and other dogs that your dog means no harm and gathers important scent information (see pages 12–13).

What's my dog thinking?

Your dog will lick his nose as a calming and appeasing signal during social chats with other dogs and with you, if he's feeling excited or uncomfortable. And as dogs "see" the world through their noses, they'll often do a full nose lick to moisten this crucial tool, allowing scent particles to stick to it so that they can "see" clearly. Lip licking is a "ritualized" or softened form of nose licking that dogs also use to say a range of things, like "I love you," "I'm sorry," "Chill out," or "No thanks." Briefly flicking the tongue gathers extra scent, too.

Bless you!

Sneezing also has a mixed function for dogs. Sneezes to clear an irritant are easy to spot, as the dog will throw his head down and pull the same squinty face as we do before sneezing. Dogs may also do smaller, ritualized sneezes to communicate during negotiations or play; these can have various meanings, from "What's that?" to "Huh, whatever."

What should I do?

In the moment:

- **Look for other body language** clues while your dog licks his nose or lips. Ears pulled back and "hard" or bulbous, staring eyes can mean he's uncomfortable or anxious; ears forward and soft eyes may mean "Please can I have that treat?"
- **Give your dog some space** if you, someone else, or another dog is in his face. He may be trying to say he's feeling crowded.

In the long term:

- **Lip lick back at your dog** now and again to say the same things to him. Dogs understand this signal and appreciate you mirroring their behavior and "talking" Dog.
- **Occasional, brief licks** of the nose and lips are normal, but if your dog licks on repeat, something is distressing him. Take note of situations in which this happens to work out what's causing it.

Ears forward, interested in what you're up to

Relaxed facial muscles and soft eyes say, "I'm feeling okay"

Tongue flicks up to wet the nose and ask, "What?"

> 66
>
> Cameras can be intimidating for dogs, so it's often hard to get a good picture without a characteristic nose lick stealing the limelight.
>
> 99

My dog rolls onto her back

My fur baby loves me tickling her tummy, and even when she meets total strangers, she often rolls over for them. Does she want a fuss from them as well?

What's my dog thinking?

Your dog uses the belly-up "Hello!" posture to say she knows *you* love her and she wants *your* attention! Dogs do roll over as a gesture of trust, but more often, it's to show they feel vulnerable. Watch your dog's body language carefully when she rolls, especially for other people; it's more likely she's asking *not* to be touched. Puppies first learn the submissive "Hands off!" roll to offer respect to adult dogs and tell new friends they're no threat—showing their precious belly leaves them open to attack and is Dog for "Don't hurt me!" (see pages 150–151).

> **"**
>
> Rolling over is a request for space rather than an invitation for you to touch the dog—unless you're already good friends!
>
> **"**

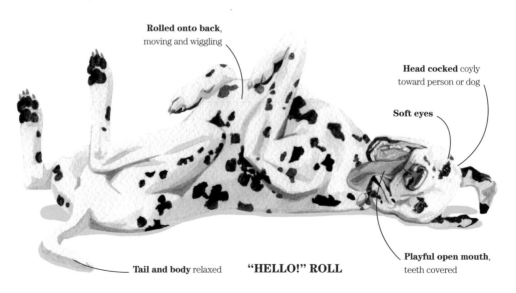

Rolled onto back, moving and wiggling

Head cocked coyly toward person or dog

Soft eyes

Tail and body relaxed

"HELLO!" ROLL

Playful open mouth, teeth covered

Head lifted, pointing toward the "threat"

Eyes soft and blinking in appeasement

Tail tucked over anal gland

"HANDS OFF!" ROLL

Rolled onto side, ready to jump up

Ears down or back

Mouth closed, or licking nose in appeasement

the function?

Ultimately, dogs roll over because looking cute and nonthreatening could mean the difference between life and death in scary situations.

What should I do?
In the moment:

- **When any dog rolls** over—including yours—assess their posture. Are they tense or relaxed, and do they have an escape route?
- **To tickle or not to tickle?** If you don't know the dog well, don't touch them. They might be rolling over to avoid your looming hands.
- **Stand up (or step back)**, give the dog some space, and see what happens. Frightened dogs will jump back to their feet. Friendly dogs will stay on their back, wagging their tail and wiggling as if to say, "Hey you! Talk to me!"

In the long term:
Train your guests to watch for signs of your dog's discomfort and show them how to greet her—by asking her to sit and take a treat.

Biting risk

The "Hands off!" roll is one of the top three misunderstood behaviors that lead to dogs being put to sleep for biting. At first, puppies roll *because* we lean down to greet them, to appease us and ask for space—then we often touch them anyway! Most dogs learn to cope with this over time, and some learn to offer their stomach to friends they trust. But it could cause a fearful dog to bite.

My dog loves a good scratch

My dog has some impressive yoga moves—she can reach her back paw all the way up to scratch the back of her head! The vet says she's healthy, with no fleas, so why does she spend so much time scratching?

What's my dog thinking?

If dogs could say, "Awkward!", this is how they would say it. "Displacement" scratching gives your dog an easy excuse to turn her head away from intense situations. Cats, humans, and many other species do it, too. This social communication can be used to say, "I'm frustrated," "I'm confused," or "I'm a little nervous." Your dog will scratch as a stress reliever and a calming signal to say, "Um, I'm sorry, I don't speak English. Can you explain it again in Dog?" If there is no sign of fleas or physical causes, your dog is trying to tell you something, so listen up!

Sickness signal?

Excessive scratching could mean your dog has fleas. It can also be one sign of a sick dog, usually accompanied by others such as restlessness, whining, or paw chewing (see pages 136–137). Your dog may have an allergy or a deeper physical issue, like anal gland blockage or worse. Be attentive, as dogs are really good at hiding signs of sickness.

What should I do?

In the moment:

- **Wait patiently** until your dog has finished scratching. Soften your voice and use hand signals rather than words if you're training her, especially in an unfamiliar place.
- **Remove the dog** from the situation if you can, or focus her attention on a chew, to help her chill out.
- **Your dog may need your help.** If she's trying to make a new dog friend and getting blanked, throw treats into the undergrowth and play "find it" with her to get her sniffing the bushes. Sniffing is another calming signal that lets other dogs see your dog as nonthreatening and helps her make friends.

In the long term:

Note the times and places where you see your dog displacement scratching; these may be distracting or confusing environments that you can add into your training plan.

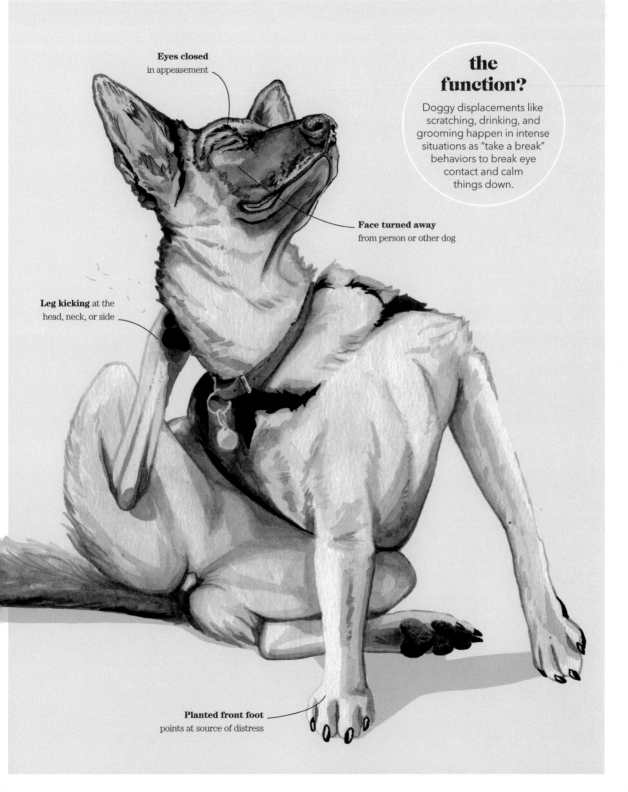

Eyes closed
in appeasement

the function?

Doggy displacements like scratching, drinking, and grooming happen in intense situations as "take a break" behaviors to break eye contact and calm things down.

Face turned away
from person or other dog

Leg kicking at the
head, neck, or side

Planted front foot
points at source of distress

SURVIVAL GUIDE

Rescuing a dog

It's incredibly rewarding to give a dog another chance at life. They get abandoned for all kinds of reasons, and the experience always takes its toll, so rescuing can often be a challenge.

1
Are *you* the one?

Most rescue dogs need some emotional rehab, and some may have deep trust issues. Some have had such a rough time that you'll have to completely adapt your lifestyle to suit their needs. Do you have the time, love, and experience they need?

2
Guard your heart

Before visiting a rescue center, think hard about what size, age, and temperament are realistic for your lifestyle. Take a wise friend, especially if you're a massive softie! If you do fall in love with a dog, visit more than once to give yourself time to be sure.

3
Listen to rescuers

Rescue staff may say a dog is not suitable for you and your family. Trust them. They know their dogs better than you do, and they want to protect them from further rejection if things don't work out in your home.

4
Give them time

Most dogs in rescue kennels are in shock and unable to show you all their beauty and complexity. Once you get them home, it can take them 3 months to fully relax. Help them by setting clear, loving boundaries on day 1.

5
Find a friend

It's natural for your new rescue dog to emotionally overattach to you. When you're away at work or on vacation, you'll need a kind and patient dogsitter or walker who understands your dog's worries.

My dog can tell time

Every day, 20 minutes before my partner comes back,
my dog looks out the window and goes to wait by the door.
It's cute ... but kind of spooky. Can she actually tell time?

What's my dog thinking?

Yes, your dog can tell time. Every living creature has a kind of internal "clock" in the brain that coordinates all their 24-hour biological cycles, or "circadian rhythms." These rhythms influence your dog's daily behavior patterns, including when she sleeps and when her stomach announces it's dinner time. Scientists have found that dogs also measure time through changes in scent—a stronger smell indicates a more recent event and a weaker smell means more time has passed. In one experiment, an owner's recently worn T-shirt was sneaked into the house to fool their dog into sleeping rather than awaiting their return as usual. Crafty scientists!

What should I do?

In the moment:
If your dog gets anxious or hyperactive before her favorite person comes home, offer some training, a snuffle mat, or a stuffed food toy before she starts fretting to take her mind off the distress of waiting.

In the long term:
- **Consistent routines** can be really calming, especially for a new rescue or a temporary guest. Fixed dinner times and similar walk times help dogs understand when they can relax and stop them from being hypervigilant (see pages 46–47).
- **Put your PJs into a bag**. Dog walkers or family members can open this scent parcel halfway through the day to calm dogs with separation anxiety (see pages 178–179). If you're going on vacation, create a few scent bags so your dog's carer can open one each day.

Timekeeping hero

Hachikō, a famous Japanese Akita, was owned by a professor at Tokyo University. After the professor's sudden death at work, Hachikō continued to wait at the station every day for his two-legged friend's return from work for nearly 10 years—he would leave his yard in time to meet the train his owner had returned on since he was a pup. A statue commemorating Hachikō's loyalty stands at Shibuya Station in Tokyo.

the function?

Keeping track of your movements is one of the most functional routines your dog can get into, because you control food, walks, doors, and activities.

"**She's home** any minute now!"

Ears alert to every sound outside

Eyes soft and shining with anticipation

Closed mouth brings in extra scent to the nose

Tense posture, alert to hints of your return

My dog digs and buries

When I buy my dog treats and toys, he buries them in the yard—the lawn is full of holes! He stashes them in his bed, too. Why is he such a squirrel?

What's my dog thinking?

Just as we take "doggy bags" home from restaurants, dogs want to save spare food for a rainy day. The main reason dogs bury treats and bones is to keep them for later because they're full. They also bury their favorite things. If your dog is worried someone might steal his prized possessions, a good way of keeping them safe is to store them in the ground. It's the same reason you might see him "invisi-burying" a treat on your carpet or in his bed. Bless!

Tail (and head)
lowered to avoid attention

Haunches braced
for digging power

Daily digging?

Burying is an atavistic behavior, an old habit inherited from wolf ancestors that dogs find comforting—like using a wood burner in a house with central heating. But if your dog is burying every day, it could be a sign of emotional distress. Call in a qualified dog behaviorist who uses force-free techniques if you are concerned.

the function?

In large wolf families, the only way to keep spare food safe is by burying it. Your dog's "pantry" is the yard!

40

> **"**
> Burying is common in busy households with multiple dogs or young children and can be a sign of stress.
> **"**

What should I do?

In the moment:

- **Don't follow your dog** if he's pacing and looking for a stash spot. He's trying to be sneaky!
- **Look at the environment**. Is there anything that might be making your dog feel threatened or anxious, which would stop him from enjoying the treat right now?
- **Some dogs can't handle** big treats. Imagine you're handed $10,000 in cash—wouldn't you instantly look for somewhere safe to put it? Reducing the size of the treat can actually help your dog enjoy it more.

In the long term:
Give your dog a sandbox to dig and bury in so he can redirect this natural behavior. Praise him when he uses it!

Brow furrowed
in concentration

Toy in mouth
for safekeeping

My dog has a crazy half-hour

Every day, once we're home from work and we've eaten dinner, my dog runs around the house like she's possessed. It's hilarious, and she seems to love it!

What's my dog thinking?

Probably "Ready? Set? *Go!*" It's so joyful watching a dog in full "zoom" mode darting at light speed from one side of your home or yard to the other, or in circles or crazy patterns, with no apparent care for their physical safety. This bizarre explosion of energy happens to some dogs daily and to others occasionally, while some live their whole lives without experiencing it. It's usually a reaction to something exciting happening or something scary—like a bath—ending. It may also be a sign that a dog needs more exercise or mental stimulation.

Tail flying high to balance sprints and quick turns

Curved, nonthreatening play posture

Frapping chaos

Scientists call this behavior "frapping," from the acronym for "frenetic random activity period," which is basically a clever way of saying crazy half-hour. Dogs are likely to nip and jump up while zooming, and also to pay no attention to previously established rules, like staying off the sofa!

> 66
>
> The dog zoom is pure heart-pounding, blood-racing joy, and one of Mother Nature's most beautiful adrenaline rushes.
>
> 99

"Play flashing" of eyes signals playful exuberance

Appeasement grinning: "I'm no threat!"

the function?

Zooming is an outpouring of pent-up emotional energy and an outlet if dogs are lacking in mental or physical exercise.

What should I do?

In the moment:

- **Open doors** and give your dog space to dash around to avoid breakages or injury. Avoid chasing or shouting, or you'll encourage the hairy hurricane.
- **Enjoy it!** Your dog is stretching all her muscles and showing you some serious hyper-play body language.
- **If your dog gets carried away** and is barking and nipping, snap her out of zooming with an enthusiastic "What's this?" and throw a treat or toy so she can focus her energy on that instead.

In the long term:

- **Give your dog** plenty of physical and mental exercise every day to keep this coiled-spring effect from happening when you want to relax.
- **Gently socialize your pup** to new things using treats to avoid something new suddenly spooking her into zooming.

SURVIVAL GUIDE

Buying a puppy

*A puppy! So cute. So loving. So many things to teach them.
So much time commitment and responsibility. Buying
a puppy is a big decision. Are you sure you're ready?*

1
Worth waiting

From the day you decide you want a puppy, wait at least 6 months before you get one. Pups are a 15-year commitment, and you'll be bringing home a baby. They take 4 months to settle in and 18 months to train.

2
Pay for advice

To find the ideal breed of dog for your lifestyle and family and to get vital tips about buying a pup safely, book a prepuppy consultation with a qualified dog behavior specialist who uses force-free techniques.

3
One at a time

Avoid buying two pups from the same litter. At around 8 weeks, pups will start learning to "speak" human and bonding to you. If they stay together, they will be lazy learners and often teach each other bad habits.

4
Age matters

Eight to 12 weeks is the ideal age to bring a puppy home, ready to start learning in your unique environment. Avoid buying a pup that is 16 weeks or older; by this age, they will have missed the sensitive phase of their development, which will lead to behavioral problems in the future.

5
Prove the price tag

What makes a pup expensive? Care; health-checked parents; and lots of early socialization to sights, sounds, and touch. Check that you're getting everything you're paying for by interviewing the breeder in their home, and make sure you see all the pups with their mom there.

My dog watches "window TV"

My dog spends all day staring out of the window. He's a nosy neighbor and watches every cat, dog, and person that passes by! Is he happy, bored, or just curious?

What's my dog thinking?

You have a self-appointed security guard. This can be a problematic "career" for a dog, even though humans have encouraged these traits in Guarding breeds (see pages 14–15). Hyper-alert dogs may stare out of the window, whimpering and twitching their head as if they're watching tennis. They may "shout" at passers-by or grumble at them under their breath, head-butt the window or the actual TV, and even body check your guests! This behavior shouldn't be laughed off. Left to practice his paranoia, the look-out dog can quickly become reactive to animals and people when he meets them.

Hypertension

Hypervigilance can quickly become a way of life. Dogs that are constantly looking for danger or threats are being drenched with stress hormones. This will shorten their lifespan, batter their immune system, and create digestive issues. You need to show them how to take time off work.

What should I do?

In the moment:
Unless your dog is peacefully watching the world go by, call him away from the window and give him a more relaxing source of entertainment, like a stuffed food toy.

In the long term:
- **Don't let him practice** being a look-out every day. Move furniture away from the window, shut the curtains, or keep him out of the "TV" room when you're out or busy.
- **Your pup needs a new occupation** and daily brain games to help him relax. Make sure he gets regular walks and training sessions to burn his mental energy, and offer him interactive puzzle toys and games where he has to work out how to get a reward. Dogs love problem solving, and if you don't give them puzzles, they'll create their own.

Brow furrowed in concentration

Eyes fixed, assessing potential threats

Mouth closed to draw in scent

Ears forward, alert

Muscle tension in shoulders

Legs braced, ready to manage danger

> 66
>
> Protecting his territory is noble work, but we have CCTV and alarms now, so tell this dog he can take a break.
>
> 99

the function?

Being a look-out is an essential job in the dog family tree. Alerting your family to all possible dangers is crucial for everyone's survival.

My dog smiles

I couldn't believe it when my dog smiled at me the other day, so I got a photo. Then a friend saw it and said she looks weird, so now I'm confused. Can dogs smile?

the function?

Smiling is a gun show. Dogs show teeth to remind you they have a mouth full of weapons and will use them if you come any closer.

What's my dog thinking?

In the entire animal kingdom, only humans show teeth to express joy. For every other species, the sight of teeth is a serious warning. (Although many selfies prove that a toothy grimace is as much of a threatening gesture for humans as it is for our monkey cousins!) Dogs can be taught that showing teeth as a greeting signal can make humans coo and give them treats, but it's important to remember that if a dog "smiles" at you, it may be for one reason … to ask you to kindly back off.

Wolf grin

Some dogs can also pull off what looks like a smile by curling the corners of their mouths up, panting gently, and squinting their eyes closed. In wolf families, this "grin" is an appeasement gesture used to keep the peace. You do it, too, when someone is staring at you.

What should I do?

In the moment:

- **If you see an Elvis-style lip curl** or full teeth, step back immediately. By doing this, you teach your dog that this behavior works rather than encouraging her to move further up a "ladder of aggression" to biting (see pages 150–151).
- **Make sure children understand** and respect this important signal to give the dog some space.

In the long term:

- **By understanding** a dog's sequence of responses, you can train your dog to ask for space in less intense ways, like head turns and lip licks (see pages 150–151).
- **Respect dogs' space** and give them alone time when they show you they need it. Your dog may not want a cuddle right now, but she'll let you know when she does.

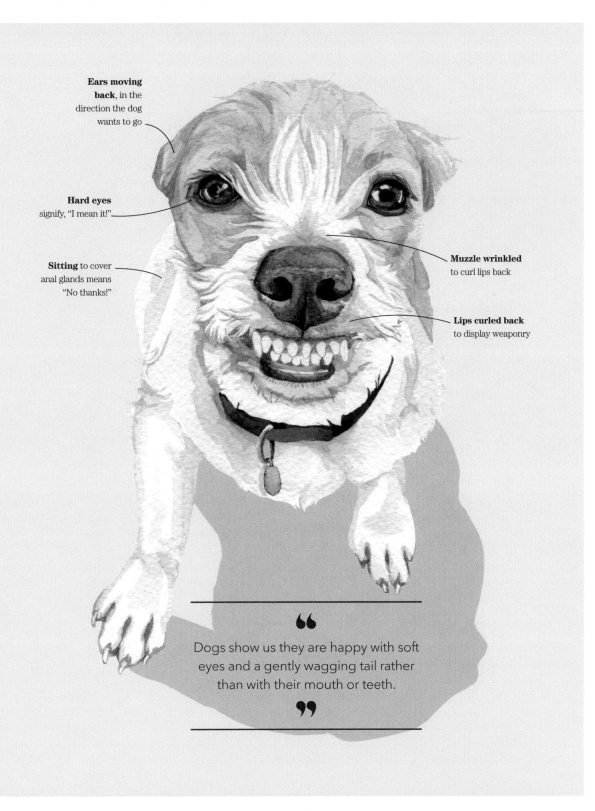

Ears moving back, in the direction the dog wants to go

Hard eyes signify, "I mean it!"

Sitting to cover anal glands means "No thanks!"

Muzzle wrinkled to curl lips back

Lips curled back to display weaponry

66

Dogs show us they are happy with soft eyes and a gently wagging tail rather than with their mouth or teeth.

99

My dog is obsessed with balls

My dog could literally play with a tennis ball every minute of the day and never get tired of it. It's great that he's so energetic, although I do wonder if it's good for him.

the function?

Playing with balls gets your attention, creates a social game, satisfies the dog's predatory urge, and releases lots of yummy dopamine. What's not to like?

What's my dog thinking?

This deep-seated doggy addiction derives from the "prey sequence" (see pages 104–105). By managing a ball, your pet gets the satisfaction of honing natural predatory skills. He also releases plenty of the feel-good hormone dopamine by chasing, catching, and squeezing a ball against a pressure sensor in his mouth. This can be great for recall and specialist training, like heelwork to music, flyball, and agility. But ball-obsessed dogs need extra training to help them relax before, during, and after ball play to stay sane.

> **"**
>
> If a tennis ball is the highest form of currency to your dog, make him earn every single throw.
>
> **"**

What should I do?

In the moment:

- **If you only want to train** an Olympic ball retriever, keep on throwing that ball! Otherwise, ask your dog to wait or do tricks before you throw it. This helps him practice switching from the reactive right brain to the "learning" left brain, calming him down.
- **During your walks**, put the ball away and use treats to help your dog come back to reality and see and sniff the world around him.

In the long term:

- **Encourage family, friends**, and guests not to feed your dog's habit by repetitively playing fetch in your home. They can easily wind your dog up, but can they calm him down?
- **Moderate access** to balls and use them as the amazing reward your dog thinks they are.

Blinkers on

Some highly driven dogs, including Gundog, Terrier, and Herding breeds, may focus intensely on balls or games to deal with stressful social situations. When they put their blinkers on, the real world fades out for them. In this state, even a small change happening around them could instantly flood their brain with information, leading to "out of nowhere" bites (see pages 26–27).

Tunnel vision: "I only have eyes for my ball"

Ears forward in interest

Mouth closed, showing this is serious business

Nose pointing at the ball, an invitation to play

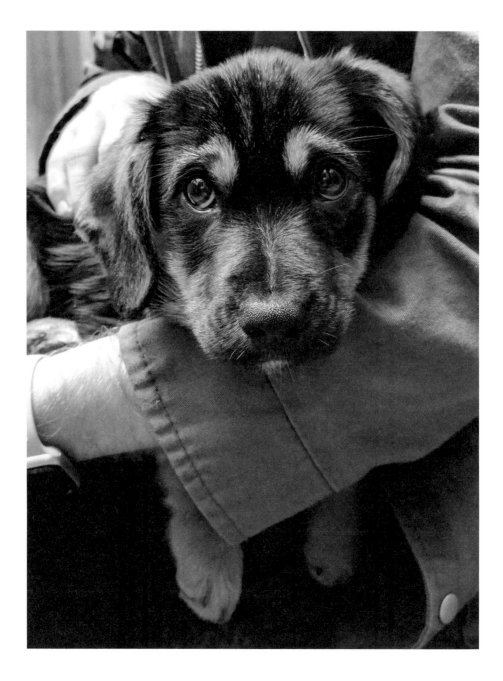

SURVIVAL GUIDE

My new dog is here!

Welcome home, doggo! It's an exciting time, but imagine how it feels to your new dog or puppy to be moving to a new home and family. Settling them in takes compassion and preparation.

1

Manage your expectations

Ah, that new dog feeling—better than Christmas, clean bedding, and the smell of fresh bread, all rolled into one! You're dreaming of long walks and cuddles in front of the fire with your new best friend, but don't forget that your dog is entering a world of unknowns and will need plenty of time, space, and understanding to settle in successfully.

2

Keep it low key

When your dog arrives, don't handle them too much, throw a family party, or let the kids bombard the dog with attention. Giving treats is a great way to make friends though.

3

One at a time

Your new dog really would prefer to explore your home one room at a time, so let them into a new room each day. After all, they're not just looking at their new surroundings—they're smelling it all in vivid detail as well.

4

Where's the potty?

On arrival, take the dog straight outside to show them where the potty is—it's only polite! Show them their "bedroom" and put a blanket with their smell on it onto the bed to help them relax. A delicious treat on the bed will help, too.

5

Easy does it

For rescue dogs, it takes 3 days to get to know their new home, 3 weeks to get to know you, and at least 3 months for you to really get to know them. Build your bond before testing it in scary places like a training class.

My dog keeps jumping up

I love that my dog is so excited when I get home; she always jumps up. But she jumps up at all my visitors, too, even ones she doesn't know, and sometimes she bounces onto me for no reason.

What's my dog thinking?

Jumping up is a signal puppies use to say, "Hello, I'm just a tiny doggo, don't hurt me." Some dogs continue doing it into adulthood to say an excited "Hi!" But jumping up can have other meanings, too. It could be that jumping gets your attention and your dog wants more of that. If she launches into you like a ninja, she may want to play. But she could also be jumping up to say, "Help me!" and escape something scary. You need to work out the function—or the *why*—of jumping up before you can decide *how* to react (see pages 22–23).

Dilated pupils: "I'm high on loving you"

Crimped "happy" ears pointing toward owner

Tongue relaxed in the mouth

Rapid tail-wagging spreads scent

Paw power

Dogs have scent glands on their feet, which leave communication pheromones everywhere they go. So jumping up and pawing you is a great way to make you smell like "family" again if you've been out without them.

HAPPY "HI!" JUMP

Whites of eyes, warning of discomfort

Ears held back in appeasement

Mouth closed indicates tension

Legs full of adrenaline, ready to flee

Tail low or tucked to hide smell "signature"

"HELP ME!" JUMP

What should I do?
Some of us actually train our dogs to jump up without realizing it. Try not to greet your dog as soon as you get home—wait until she calms down, then say hello. Greeting her on her bed will teach her to go there when people arrive.

Be your dog's safe space. Look out for things you know she finds scary—like a butt sniff or a noisy toddler—and pick her up before she jumps.

If she leaps up to demand play, don't reward her by playing.

To reduce jumping:
- **Twist your body away** when your dog jumps, so she doesn't land her paws on you.
- **Say hello** without using your hands.
- **Throw treats on the floor** when you come in to teach your dog to keep all four paws on the floor whenever people arrive.

> 66
> "Hi!" and "Help!" are two common meanings for jumping up. Look at your dog's posture, tail, ears, and eyes for clues about how she feels.
> 99

My dog spins and barks when he's excited

The second we get the lead out, begin getting his dinner ready, or go to answer the door, my dog starts spinning and barking. It's amazing, like he's worked out his own high-speed song-and-dance routine!

What's my dog thinking?

Your dog is on an energy rollercoaster and wants you to hurry up. Dogs can learn to offer this kind of behavior because it makes a walk or dinner arrive faster (see pages 162–163). It's cute when pups spin and bark, and you may have inadvertently taught your dog to do it by rewarding funny spins or twirls with treats and toys; in that case, this movement feels like pure joy to him. Some dogs spin as a mildly compulsive behavior to help them deal with the stress of waiting; they can be harder to slow down.

Human vending machines

There are lots of things we unconsciously train our dogs to do that seem fun at the time but later become irritating habits. Does your dog paw you to touch them, then paw you again when you stop? Instantly or absentmindedly rewarding this with further touch teaches them to paw guests … and strangers. Earning our attention, not expecting it automatically, has numerous benefits for dogs.

What should I do?

In the moment:

- **Stop what you're about to do**. If your dog doesn't get the reward he's anticipating, he'll want to try something new that might work instead—and you can train him to do a new trick.
- **If you're worried** your dog is stressed, refocus his hyperactivity by offering a food-based toy.

In the long term:

- **Be proactive**. Ask for an alternative behavior before your dog twirls; over time, this will replace spinning.
- **Introduce "station" training**, or mat training, so your dog learns to go to the same place and sit there on your cue.
- **Change your routines**. If you always get the lead from the same cabinet, it's no wonder your dog goes bonkers when he sees you going there. Put the lead down again, in another place sometimes, to break the association for him.

Barking with teeth covered in excitement rather than fear

Hair flying off while spinning can indicate stress and excitement

the function?

Spinning or twirling and barking is an outlet for joy, excitement, or frustration. Offer direction, or dogs will make up their own moves!

High-speed movement, fueled by frustration

66

What would you like your dog to do instead of spinning? Successfully changing behavior starts with a clear training goal.

99

My dog likes eating grass

I spend a fortune on good-quality dog food, yet every day my dog goes outside and munches on grass. My neighbor says he's trying to make himself sick. Could he have an eating disorder?

What's my dog thinking?

Your dog's behavior isn't unusual; in fact, almost all dogs eat grass. And often not just any grass, but a particular grass called "couch grass" or "dog grass." But the jury is still out as to why. We know ancestral dogs hunted herbivores in the wild and often ate their grass-filled stomach contents first. Dogs also love eating herbivore droppings, which are basically grass. They'll often eat grass after a stressful social encounter, which suggests it may also help them relax or combat a feeling of sickness or anxiety. Sometimes they will eat grass in groups, a bit like sharing nuts at the bar!

Doggy detox?

Alongside chlorophyll, couch grass contains triticin, mucilage, potassium, zinc, and agropyrene oil, which have potent antibiotic properties that fight infection and help dissolve bladder or kidney stones. It has also long been used as a human herbal remedy (or "spring tonic") by the Swiss and French to detox the kidney and liver.

What does it mean?

No one knows for sure. One theory is that couch grass is long enough to bind up worms in the gut, helping dogs get rid of parasites naturally. Another suggests that it tickles the back of the throat and helps a dog be sick if they need to.

Grass may supplement missing nutrients. It contains chlorophyll (the green bit in plants), which can improve the health of the blood, helping fight infection and liver cancers, and aid digestion. Modern dogs can't choose their diets, and very few dog foods include fresh green vegetables. Mixing parboiled greens like kale, broccoli, and spinach with regular food will do them good.

One scientific study found that nearly 80 percent of owners said their dogs ate grass every day, while only 8 percent were sick afterward. So don't worry—eating grass doesn't necessarily mean that a dog has an urge to purge.

> Around 80 percent of dogs and 47 percent of wolves eat grass daily, so it's not only natural, it's highly likely to be nutritional.

Closed eyes and relaxed ears signify enjoyment

Chewing with back molars releases the feel-good hormone dopamine

Couch grass has thick, long blades

the function?

Lack of nutrients? Added roughage? Antacid? Purging agent? Maybe couch grass is just plain delicious! More research is needed to discover why dogs eat grass.

SURVIVAL GUIDE

Socializing a puppy

It's time for your puppy to discover roads, kids, soccer balls, hats, cats, and more! Lack of socialization is the main reason young dogs get abandoned, so don't delay showing your pup the world.

1
Get your plan in place
Socializing a puppy is time sensitive. You should introduce your pup to everything they will need to be confident around as an adult, when they are between 8 and 16 weeks old. That's just 2 months to cram in all kinds of different experiences, so start planning those training day trips!

2
Build positive associations
Socialization is the process of becoming confident around different sights, sounds, textures, and smells and learning appropriate behavior in different situations. Taking delicious treats out with you will help your puppy build positive associations with lots of different environments.

3
Play safe
You need to be able to spot the signs of both fair and unfair play (see pages 120–121 and 122–123) before you allow your young puppy to play with other dogs, so you can properly supervise their playtime.

4
Hands-off learning
Keeping the lead loose is crucial during socialization. If pups are experiencing something new, you can spook them and even create phobias by pulling their lead tight or overhandling them.

5
Create a den
It can all get a bit much sometimes. Tired pups will frequently need to rest and retreat, just like human babies, so give them somewhere quiet where they can hide and feel safe.

My dog is a humper

I don't understand why my cheeky boy is always humping. I've neutered him, but he still does it to other dogs and at home to couch cushions, toys, the cat … and me! Is he trying to be pack leader?

What's my dog thinking?

Let's not overcomplicate this—he's thinking it feels nice! Humping is a sexual behavior that is also a common response to anxiety or frustration in any situation; it works quickly to give your dog a sense of pleasure and control when he might be feeling a bit stressed. Both males and females hump, even after being neutered or spayed. And contrary to popular belief, humping has nothing to do with so-called dominance; in fact, frequent humpers aren't usually the most confident dogs. Believe it or not, they're often trying to calm themselves or the other dog by humping them.

What should I do?

In the moment:
- **Don't shout at your dog**, as this will reinforce the behavior. Calmly walk out of the room or remove your attention to show him you're not impressed.
- **When your dog looks wired** and ready to hump, redirect him onto a chew to self-soothe, which is far more socially acceptable.
- **Call your dog away** if he sticks his head over another dog's back when they meet—it could signal he's about to hump. Socially anxious dogs might do this after a greeting or if they're feeling threatened (pages 116–119).

In the long term:
Note the context to figure out why your dog feels the need to hump. Does it happen when your favorite TV show has just started, someone new has come in, or something has been taken away from him?

Should I neuter?

It's a common misconception, even among some vets, that humping will be reduced by neutering or spaying because it's mostly a sexually driven or dominant behavior (see pages 24–25). There is zero scientific evidence that neutering improves any behavior except roaming—that is, running off after unspayed females in heat. Neutering won't stop dogs humping, and may even increase aggression in nervous dogs, who would prefer others don't get close enough to discover their reproductive status by butt-sniffing them.

" Self-assured dogs don't go around humping everything. A truly confident dog doesn't need to—their posture and scent say it all for them. "

Ears pull back as the brain says, "Move back a bit and down a bit"

Tail and tongue curled in concentration

Front legs clamp to hold the "victim"

the function?

Humping has a sexual function, and it's also an easy way for any dog to express themselves and self-soothe if they're feeling frustrated or anxious.

My dog is a social media star

My dog is a star! She has a huge social media following and a bigger wardrobe than I do. People love watching her pose like a queen and I love being her tour manager.

What's my dog thinking?

It's wonderful to think the world loves your dog as much as you do, and who doesn't want a fan club for their best friend? But it's easy to become addicted to the likes and get carried away with dressing up your furry friend. Some dogs enjoy having your full attention while you get snap happy, but most will feel intimidated by being put into a tutu or a top hat. Watch your dog's body language for clues; she may be feeling stressed and thinking, "I'd take a park walk over the catwalk any day!"

What should I do?

If you need to hold your dog to dress her, she probably isn't very comfortable with it. If she pants or freezes, she's definitely stressed. You can teach dogs to enjoy wearing costumes using treats and patience (see pages 172–173), but if your dog pulls away, stop and let her escape.

Think about the breed and coat. Dogs with thick double coats will overheat in a puffer jacket or pullover.

> 66
>
> Are the accessories for your dog, or has the dog become your accessory? Dogs' beauty is more than skin deep.
>
> 99

"Fashion" accessories could also be uncomfortable—and giving your dog a glow stick necklace sounds like fun, until she pulls it off and chews it!

Spending more time on your dog's social media account than interacting with her? Consider an extra hour a day of play, training, or walks instead.

Poking fun

Dogs know when you're laughing at them. Like us, dogs are social creatures that empathize with friends' feelings and facial expressions and learn by imitation. Dressing dogs up to look "funny" may not only make them feel sad, it also encourages the next generation to poke fun at them, too. Is that the kind of influencer you want to be?

the function?

Bonding over bandannas or pimping your puppy—what's the function for *you* of dressing up your dog, and is she happy to go along with it?

Frown lines indicate tension

Ears back, worrying about what's on her

Whites of eyes suggest discomfort

Panting to relieve stress

Footwear covers scent glands and may cause overheating

My dog sniffs absolutely everything

My dog spends the whole walk sniffing. It's like he's an art connoisseur and there's a Mona Lisa at the bottom of every lamppost that needs a thorough inspection, every single day. What's so fascinating?

What's my dog thinking?

For your dog, stopping at a regular sniff spot is a bit like you checking your social media. Dogs' incredibly sensitive noses and scent organs can "read" updates from other animals about the time of their visit and direction of travel and identify their species, age, reproductive status, stress levels, diet, and health—all from a trickle of urine. He may even lift a leg to "like" a post and add to the "chat"! Deep dives on these forums take time, so respect this world of scent—but don't let it rule your walks.

Calm it down

Sniffing is also a calming signal, which is something dogs use to ask people and other dogs to relax. If we're yanking, rushing, or stressing at our dogs, they may keep their nose to the ground or suddenly dart off somewhere for a good sniff to defuse mounting tension. Check how you're feeling and, if you want your dog's attention, turn that frown upside down! (See pages 92–93 and 168–169.)

What should I do?

In the moment:

- **Four's fair!** Invite your dog to sniff every fourth sniff spot by giving the "Go see" cue. Allow him 2–5 minutes of deep sniffing there.
- **When time's up, go**. Walk on confidently with a cue like "This way!" and treat and praise your dog for coming, too. If you cajole him too gently to keep walking, chances are he'll totally ignore you.

In the long term:

- **At the park**, play a fun game of detective with your dog to channel his sniffing. Run ahead of him and plant a treat in a tuft of grass; then wait there, looking down, until he arrives to inspect the "find." Quickly run somewhere else and do the same again.
- **Do an occasional walk** entirely dedicated to sniffing. Teaching obedience games will help your dog check in with you during these sniff walks.

SURVIVAL GUIDE

Walking the dog

You'll definitely get more exercise! But walking your dog can be a dream or a nightmare, depending on your outlook and how much treat-based training you do to build a relationship down the lead.

1
Do it daily
Unless your dog is reactive or scared, walk them outside daily to stop them from going stir-crazy. Regularly walked dogs are more able to relax when left and remain well socialized with the world.

2
Plan for fun
Take treats and toys to build good times and happy memories. You wouldn't take the kids to the park without a soccer ball or a frisbee, so go out planning to have just as much fun with your dog.

3
Grab the moment
Take your earphones out and put your phone in your pocket. Being present with your dog on walks means you can enjoy their antics, keep them safe, and build a stronger bond.

4
Mix it up
Vary your route and style to keep walks exciting. Do a road walk one day, then a walk in the park, then a training walk, and then maybe a sensory "sniffing" walk, or even some urban parkour!

5
Comfy clothes
Use a broad, padded collar or harness with a buckle to walk your dog. Choke chains, slip leads, and martingale collars cause pain and will make everything on the walk unpleasant for them.

6
Stay loose
Training your dog to walk on a loose lead can reduce their reactivity to other dogs and people, which means walks are better for everyone. (See pages 170–171.)

CHAPTER TWO

Me and my amazing dog

Building a deep, lifelong bond with a dog is such a rewarding experience. Our dogs are always showing us we're the center of their world—even if we misunderstand their methods sometimes.

My dog melts me with a look

Whenever I'm eating, I look down and there's a little face with big eyes that I can't resist. Where's the harm in giving my poor hungry girl an extra sausage— or two—off of my plate?

the function?

Domesticated dogs that appealed more to humans got better food more often, allowing them to thrive, have more pups, and pass on the "cute gene."

What's my dog thinking?

There's no mistaking this posture—it's pure, unadulterated "Pleeease?" Dogs use a particular facial muscle to raise their inner eyebrows, making their eyes look bigger and more childlike. One research study found that dogs evolved this muscle over thousands of years of domestication, specifically to appeal to humans and to prompt us to offer care. Context is key here; your dog may just want food, a walk, or some attention. She could also be trying to soothe you or genuinely feeling anxious (pp.64–65, 178–179).

> 66
> Big eyes, together with dogs' domed heads, mimic the look of a human baby, which triggers the same nurturing instinct in us.
> 99

What should I do?

In the moment:

- **Look away from puppy eyes** if you don't want your dog to beg for treats or attention. Eye contact is her greatest prize, and she'll do more of whatever she's doing if you reward her with it.
- **If your dog is scared** and asking for help, respond. But if she just wants food or affection, tough love is usually the better option.

In the long term:

- **Train everyone**—you too, Grandpa!—not to treat the dog for making puppy eyes when they're eating. One person giving in will train her to beg from everyone.
- **Put well-being first**. Treating your dog for looking cute feels good and may strengthen your bond, but it isn't really love. Will you do the extra-long walks needed to work off her widening waistline?

Domed head helps make most dogs look babylike

Wide, big eyes say, "Love me"

Sad face

Although we're quick to put human emotions onto pets, the guilty-looking dog is a myth (pages 24–25). Everything dogs do is either functional or not functional for them, so they have no sense of right and wrong. But they will learn that a sad face appeases you if you're complaining or pointing, because they've done something you don't like. Don't punish a "guilty" face—dogs don't "know" what they've done.

Ears forward, framing the face for maximum cuteness

My dog licks my face

My dog licks disgusting things and then kisses me! I don't mind, as I know it's love, but I draw the line when he tries to cover kids with slobber.

the function?

For dogs, face licking is a sign of affection, respect, and appeasement and a chance to gather information or beg for food.

What's my dog thinking?

Your dog is saying he loves you while also seeking information from pheromones in saliva and from glands around the mouth to work out how you're feeling. It's also a great way of covering your face in his unique smell. Puppies perform this important ritual during weaning, because face licking stimulates parents to regurgitate semidigested meat for them—a bit like a toddler diving into shopping bags when their parents get home. Be cautious though: bacteria in dog saliva could include Salmonella and harmful strains of E. coli.

Doggy diagnosis?

Medical detection dogs prove that our incredible dogs can smell the odor signature of physical issues ranging from blood sugar levels to cancer. Dogs' super-sensitive noses are so used to smelling us every day, they are likely to sniff, paw, or lick us excessively when they smell a change that might signal a health problem.

What should I do?

In the moment:

- **It's your choice**, but laughing or praising your dog for face licking will encourage a full face wash!
- **If someone doesn't like** being licked, ask them not to make a fuss, as your dog will probably want to lick them even more to show he's no threat. Get them to move away and show the dog they're not interested.

In the long term:

- **If there are people** you don't want your dog to lick, it's best not to let him practice on you.
- **Going face to face** is a confrontational situation for a dog. Thankfully, most give a loving lick when we get too close, but children who enjoy face licks at home could make a dangerous mistake by sticking their face too close to unknown dogs.

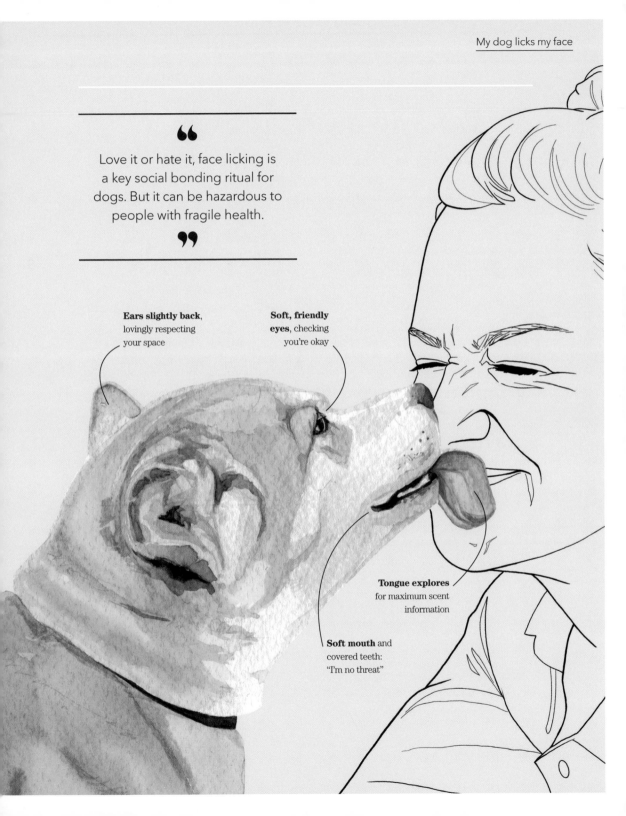

" Love it or hate it, face licking is a key social bonding ritual for dogs. But it can be hazardous to people with fragile health. "

Ears slightly back, lovingly respecting your space

Soft, friendly eyes, checking you're okay

Tongue explores for maximum scent information

Soft mouth and covered teeth: "I'm no threat"

My dog yawns in my face

Every day my dog comes up for cuddles, but after 5 minutes,
she yawns right in my face. Is she trying to say she's bored of me?

What's my dog thinking?

Yes, she thinks you're boring! Only kidding. Truth is, your dog could be saying lots of different things by yawning. Yawns can mean "Hello," "Hurry up," "Help," "I can't wait," "I'm so excited," "I don't want that," "I don't understand," or "What are we doing next?" Dogs will often yawn as a subconscious displacement behavior and a calming signal, which they use in times of gentle stress to defuse tension (see pages 22–23). Yawning also has an important biological function for your dog, preparing her for action by taking in oxygen to fuel the brain and muscles.

Two-way conversation

Yawning is one of a number of cross-species behaviors used by both humans and dogs to express frustration, distress, or anticipation—so when you yawn, your dog could very well be wondering, "What's my human thinking?" If you yawn and stretch near a friendly dog, they'll often approach and lick your face to say hello, because you're speaking Dog!

What should I do?

In the moment:

- **Don't yawn-spoil** by putting your finger in the dog's mouth. It's mean!
- **Zoom out** and look at the context. Is your dog anticipating something fun, scary, or frustrating or telling you something is happening to or around her that's mildly stressful? (See pages 20–21.)
- **Listen when she yawns**. Is there a squeak or a sigh, too? Dogs often combine yawning with vocal work for added dramatic effect to get you to act in a certain way or to get your attention—for example, if they are waiting for you to walk them.

In the long term:

- **Teach family and friends** to recognize this gentle stress signal and respond compassionately to your dog's request for a change, maybe by opening a door or releasing her from a hug.
- **Notice the pattern** of your dog's yawns. Is there a common theme, like the presence of a dog in the park you thought was her buddy but is actually a "frenemy"?

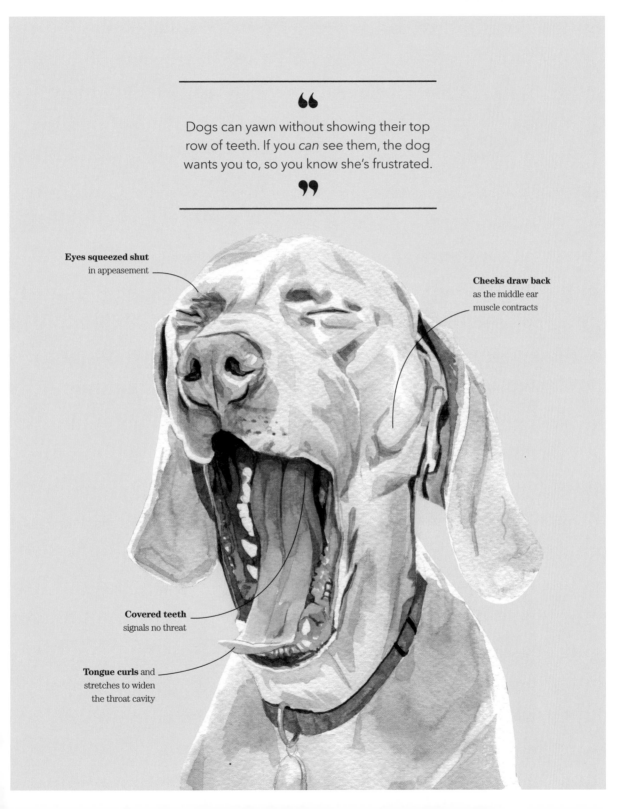

> 66
>
> Dogs can yawn without showing their top row of teeth. If you *can* see them, the dog wants you to, so you know she's frustrated.
>
> 99

Eyes squeezed shut
in appeasement

Cheeks draw back
as the middle ear
muscle contracts

Covered teeth
signals no threat

Tongue curls and
stretches to widen
the throat cavity

SURVIVAL GUIDE

Walking in town

Whether you're a cosmopolitan shopaholic or a rural dweller, teaching your best friend to watch and trust you on busy streets is crucial for pups and great distraction training for older dogs!

1
All about timing
Quickly treat and praise your dog whenever they're spooked by strange sights like bikes or buses. Capturing the moment they react with a "Whoa!" and turning it into "Yay!" will reduce their anxiety.

2
Take a breather
If your dog is looking stressed by the hustle and bustle of town life, divert down a quiet side road to reduce the level of distraction and let them do some relaxed sniffing instead.

3
Baby steps
Take your time when first taking a puppy somewhere built-up and busy. Keep your training sessions in intense environments short—a maximum of 10–15 minutes at first—then build that up.

4
Keep treats close
As you walk, have a tasty treat ready and keep it close to your dog's nose to help them safely pass people and other dogs on narrower parts of the pavement.

5
Breezy does it
Keep your lead loose and your tone light to show your dog that you enjoy being in these strange and busy places, so they can enjoy it, too! (See pages 26–27 and 170–171.)

6
Are we there yet?
Work toward a rewarding goal, like a visit to the pet store, a dog-friendly café, or another regular pitstop, where your dog can enjoy a chew or snack. They'll remember it the next time!

My dog looks ready to pounce on me

Sometimes at home my pooch goes downward dog on her elbows as if she's going to pounce on me, and she does it with other dogs at the park, too. Are they playing or fighting?

What's my dog thinking?

This friendly move is a permission-seeking pose that's Dog for "What do you want to play?" Pouncing with elbows down and butt raised to the sky is one of the nicest ways your dog can invite another dog—or you—to build a deeper bond with them through play (see pages 116–119). It also tells playmates that whatever happens next, it's not serious. Dogs are so skilled at keeping the peace, sometimes they'll play bow when a stressed-out dog greets them a bit too intensely, as a kind of comic distraction to calm the other dog.

the function?

For dogs, the main function of play bowing is to say, "I'm ready for some good, old-fashioned fun; care to join me in a game?"

Relaxed, happy facial expression says, "I'm chill! Let's play!"

Posture: a ritualized prey bow, as if saying, "En garde!"

Wagging tail in a neutral position shows the dog isn't overaroused

Downward dog shows off the dog's age, energy, and flexibility

What should I do?

In the moment:

- **Play bow back to your dog!**
  Bowing is a behavior dogs can easily read, and they love it when you do it to them.
- **Call your dog away** if she is off lead and play bows at another dog that is on a lead, or they could both get frustrated that they aren't able to play together.

In the long term:

Use play bows and other play signals to recall your dog away from other dogs—for sociable dogs, play is much more valuable than treats. Hold a treat in one hand, call your dog, then swing that hand from high above your head, down to your toes. She'll think you're in a great mood and inviting her into a fun game!

Prey or play?

A "prey bow" happens just before a dog pounces on prey and is a natural instinct (see pages 104–105). Play and prey bows look similar, because a play bow is a prey bow in "ritualized" form. Ritualized behaviors are simplified or softened versions of important survival skills adapted over time for a social function. So play bows are a gentler version of a deadly serious hunting move, similar to children play fighting with pretend swords.

My dog pees when I get home

I love getting home to greet my pup, but our big reunion is always spoiled by him peeing on the floor—and all over me!

the function?

Urine contains messages about a dog's age and sexual maturity. Bladder emptying is a quick way for pups to say, "Hello! I'm young, be nice to me!"

What's my dog thinking?

Your dog is either celebrating your arrival with a pee party, or he might be worried about being handled. Puppies have a faster metabolism than older dogs and less control over the sphincter that connects to their bladder, so they're more likely to pee the moment they're excited or stressed. Also, puppies have tiny bladders: a Labrador's is around the size of a lemon and a Yorkshire Terrier's is the size of a large grape. That's why it's important while you're potty training to take your pup outside on the hour, every hour.

Run ... for the bathroom!

Ever played hide and seek and suddenly realized you're desperate for the bathroom? Adrenaline tells the body to quickly shed any unnecessary weight, in case you need to run for your life. Sudden bursts of intense joy or fear produce the same response in a dog.

What should I do?

In the moment:

- **Expect a fountain** from your young pup when you first get home, and take him straight outside so he can learn that he'll get praised for outdoor pees.
- **Don't scold your dog** for greeting pees, or this response may become ingrained in the dog into adulthood.
- **Try not to loom**, because leaning over young dogs—especially in an enclosed hallway—can cause them to pee in submission. If your dog is nervous or rolls over, greet him by kneeling down or throw a ball to focus your greeting elsewhere.

In the long term:

Get a vet checkup on adult dogs that are still peeing when you get home, as this may be a sign of a urinary tract infection or even kidney dysfunction or diabetes.

Eyes soft in friendly appeasement

Mouth open, panting in excitement

Crimped "happy" ears invite touch

High tail in greeting shows arousal

> 66
>
> Your puppy will eventually grow out of peeing "Hello!" Until then, keep your greeting tone calm and the paper towel on standby!
>
> 99

My dog brings me a present when I come home

When I arrive home—or anyone else comes round—my dog always finds a present to bring: shoes, toys, and even her bed. Then she won't actually give it up when I say, "Drop!"

What's my dog thinking?

This is one of the cutest human–dog misconceptions. Believe it or not, holding an item helps relax some dogs and has little to do with offering you something. When excitement hits, a switch deep in the dog's brain flips and says, "I have to *hold* something!" And because the sight of you (and your visitors) makes your dog so excited, she needs a pacifier to help her cope with the feeling. So don't take her "gift" away—she needs it! You'll most often see this "toy parade" coping strategy in fetch-and-carry Gundog breeds (see pages 14–15).

> **"**
>
> Gift-bringers clamp onto any nearby item and have little to no awareness of what it is; they *can't*, rather than won't, drop it.
>
> **"**

What should I do?

In the moment:

- **Praise your dog** for carrying the item, but don't take it from her. As soon as your dog calms down, she'll naturally relax her jaw and let it go.
- **If the item could be harmful** to your dog, calmly call her and hold a treat by her nose so she can choose to swap it. Have an alternative ready—like a toy— in case she needs a replacement to soothe her.
- **Don't chase your dog** or scold her for "choosing" the item. This could ruin your bond, stop her fetching, and teach her to guard by swallowing (see pages 140–141).

In the long term:

You can train gift-bringers to fetch something you *do* want, like slippers, by practicing "find it" and fetch games with that item using treats and toys. Then keep treats by the front door and when you arrive home, send your pupper to "Go find!"

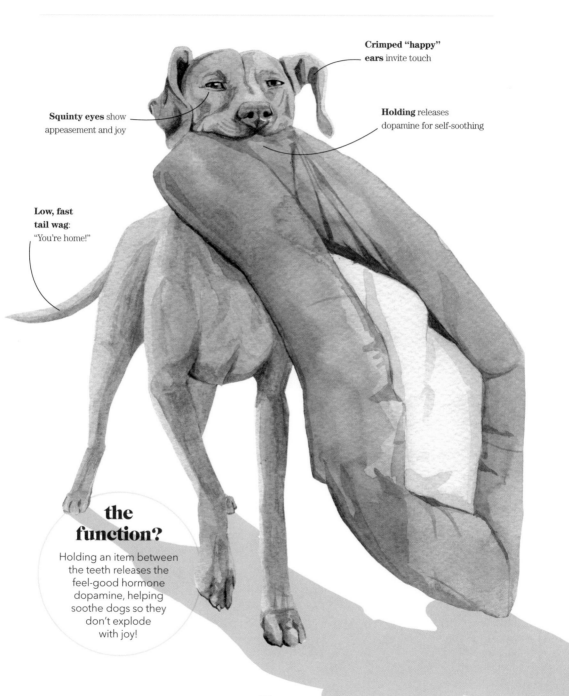

Crimped "happy" ears invite touch

Squinty eyes show appeasement and joy

Holding releases dopamine for self-soothing

Low, fast tail wag: "You're home!"

the function?

Holding an item between the teeth releases the feel-good hormone dopamine, helping soothe dogs so they don't explode with joy!

Leaving your puppy

Unless you're willing to quit your job and social life for good, you will need to leave your pup alone one day. Puppy parents need to teach pups how to relax on their own from a young age.

1
Daytime distractions

Make sure there are three or four things your pup can chew or snuffle while you walk away to another room. When they realize they can't get to you, they may whimper, but they'll quickly reengage with their toys. This is your cue to return! Your pup has now learned that chewing and playing is a good way to ensure you come back, which is what you want them to do when you leave.

2
Build up slowly

The best time to practice daytime separation is when your puppy has had exercise, mental stimulation, and something to eat. You should increase these separation periods gradually, over at least 2 months. If you find that your pup is destroying their pen, the doors, or the baseboards in frustration, it means you're going away for too long, too quickly.

3
Sleep apart

From day 1, have your pup sleep in a crate or pen in a different room to you overnight to get them used to a good 6–8 hours alone for sleeping.

4
Leave them to cry?

Experts used to advise letting puppies cry at night, but it is important they know you're there to keep them safe and secure. During the night, you can go back in and settle a crying puppy, but then head straight back to bed again. Stick at it, and your pup will eventually drop off to sleep!

My dog gets jealous

My dog is so jealous! When I'm sitting on the couch, he pushes my partner and my cat out of the way to get onto my lap, then he won't let them get near me.

What's my dog thinking?

Jealousy is a combination of love, fear, and frustration, from your dog's perspective, and his past experience of sharing you will affect his behavior in the future. We can con ourselves into thinking this behavior is sweet or funny, but the truth is your dog is deeply insecure about losing your attention and is successfully controlling access to you. He needs reminding that he's still important to you when new people and animals come into your life, and time and training to learn that it's valuable to him to share you.

the function?

For dogs, controlling their source of food, walks, and love is crucial for survival, and if it works, they'll keep doing it (see pages 22–23).

> 66
>
> You are the center of your dog's world, but he needs your support to learn that "I want" doesn't mean he'll always get your attention.
>
> 99

What should I do?

In the moment:

Resist scolding the dog for expressing jealousy, even if he snaps, or he'll learn the presence of other people and animals means he gets told off, which will make him even more insecure.

In the long term:

- **Don't let your dog** break your attention to a loved one by taking a control position between you in bed or on the couch. If he does, calmly move him down again.
- **Make sharing your attention** valuable for your dog; always praise and treat him for being patient with the "competition."
- **Ration the affection** and physical contact you offer. Dogs that get fast, easy access to us are quick to throw a tantrum when they can't!
- **Give dogs fun things** to eat or play with in their own bed rather than letting them sit on or near you all day.

Love drug

When you gaze into your dog's eyes, your brains both produce oxytocin, the social bonding hormone. This hormone tells us to care for, comfort, and fight for one another. Oxytocin can cause some dogs to want to control access to their favorite people, even if that means making an enemy of everyone else (see pages 72–73).

Ears back, not happy at the approaching "threat"

"Enthroned" lap sitting may be love or control

Stroking the dog can reinforce his guarding behavior

My dog follows me around the house

My dog is my shadow. I work at home, so I'm with her all day, but I still can't go upstairs, put the kids to bed, or even go to the bathroom without a little tagalong following my every move.

What's my dog thinking?

Your "velcro dog" is telling you, "I love you" and "Don't leave me!" Following you from time to time is fine, but if she can't relax without being next to you, she's not okay. Dogs overattach to us to cope with feelings of anxiety that can arise when they haven't learned a proper separation routine, and—oddly enough—from us frequently petting and checking in with them. Mindlessly stroking your dog for hours or letting her warm your feet while you work makes her think you won't cope if she's not there.

Lean on you

Rescue dogs often form insecure bonds to their new human family and show this by physically leaning on them. These dogs suffer grief and trauma when they are abandoned or rehomed, so they'll stick like glue to new, loving people. Asking for touch by leaning on a family member at every opportunity is the dog's insurance policy against ending up alone again.

What should I do?

In the moment:

- **Try not to reinforce** your dog's anxious behavior pattern by constantly talking to, touching, or praising her.
- **Shut doors** after you sometimes. Dogs that are given 24/7 access to you aren't getting the chance to learn impulse control, frustration tolerance, and independence (see pages 88–89).

In the long term:

- **Take your dog** to her own bed two or three times a day and give her a big reward there, like a chew, a food-based toy, or dinner.
- **Train for time apart** by teaching "sit" and "wait" using treats. Can you go up and down the stairs or out of the room with your dog staying put?
- **Create a routine** to help your dog learn to enjoy alone time and relax while you're out or elsewhere in your home (see pages 178–179).

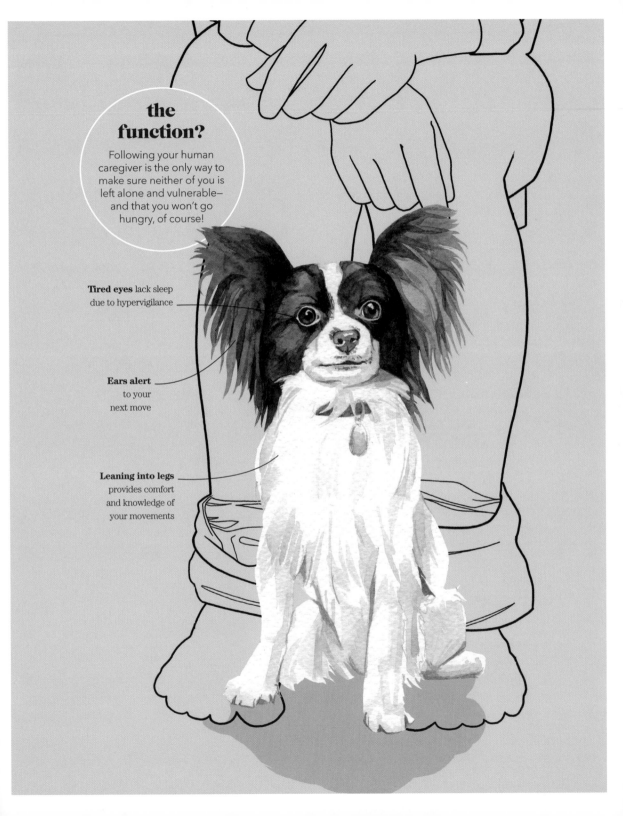

the function?

Following your human caregiver is the only way to make sure neither of you is left alone and vulnerable—and that you won't go hungry, of course!

Tired eyes lack sleep due to hypervigilance

Ears alert to your next move

Leaning into legs provides comfort and knowledge of your movements

My dog ignores me

I'm with my dog all day and I do the feeding and walking, but in the evening when everyone else gets home, my dog completely ignores me. He won't even come for a cuddle!

What's my dog thinking?

So many doggy parents feel hurt by this behavior! But your dog isn't saying he likes everyone else in your family more than you. Dogs are attracted to novelty, so when fresh faces arrive home, they will be of higher value to your dog for a while. The dog may not know you want him to come to you, or he may just not be in the mood right now, and that's okay. He may simply not understand your "come here" cue word. Try to understand your dog's point of view, and don't take this personally.

Eyes scanning for a distraction

Head turn means "No, thank you"

Open mouth and gentle panting shows relaxation

> 66
>
> Being busy, turning away from your dog, and an excited tone of voice are great for getting his attention.
>
> 99

Ears pointing in different directions suggest a motivational conflict

What should I do?

In the moment:

Play hard to get!
Spend more time focusing your love and energy on your human family so your dog has fewer opportunities to ignore you. He'll quickly become intrigued about the excitement happening around you.

In the long term:

- **Give your dog** two short clicker training sessions each day to build "conversations" into your companionship.
- **Do some recall training** so your dog understands the "come" cue.
- **Does your dog** need to be with you all day? Consider giving him some time in the day to relax away from you in another room. After all, absence does make the heart grow fonder.
  - **Get the vet** to check your dog's hearing and eyesight, as dogs' senses deteriorate with age, just like ours.

the function?

Your dog could be distracted by other people, smells, or sounds; asking you to calm down; or unsure of what you want (see pages 22–23).

Put those paws up

Some dogs spend the whole day thinking that they are looking after *you* (see pages 46–47 and 90–91). If you have a dog that wants to be your chaperone or footrest, they'll need proper rest after their long day's work. Make sure your family understand, and let your sleeping dog lie when they get home. Dogs disturbed during deep relaxation can be moody and may snap (see pages 154–155).

My dog chews my stuff

Every day there's some new carnage: whether I'm at home or at work, my dog chews up my stuff, and it's always my stuff. Now my favorite shoes are "Jimmy Chews"! What have I done to deserve this?

What's my dog thinking?

You bought a dog to reduce your stress levels, not triple your shopping bill. But this often misunderstood behavior stems from only one place: love. Dogs are drawn to the pheromones in the smell of the people they love, and your personal scent sticks to items you use a lot, like your shoes, your phone, and even the TV remote. Chewing is also a great stress reliever when your dog feels lonely, frustrated, or hyperactive: what better way to calm down than to find your favorite person's things and have a good chew on them?

Soft-eyed "joygasm" face from dopamine release

Chew pushed against molars and soft palate creates maximum enjoyment

94

Seriously? You ate my pants?

Some dogs take it a step further and will lick, chew, or even devour your underwear. That seems pretty gross to us, but for a dog, your undies are the ultimate gourmet slice of your unique musk, and they think that's delicious. We're talking about an animal that sniffs butts to say hello, don't forget.

the function?

Pressing chews against the back teeth (molars) and soft palate produces lots of the stress-relieving hormone dopamine, which is both soothing and addictive.

Lying down in curled "C" position shows comfort

What should I do?

In the moment:

- **Don't chase or scold** your dog; this could teach them that chewing will also lead to a fun game. Even worse, your dog may "guard" the chewed item by swallowing it (see pages 140–141).
- **Offer your dog a fair swap** and praise them for picking up a chew or toy instead of your slippers.

In the long term:

- **Keep important belongings** out of harm's way until your dog or puppy has learned the "leave it" or "drop" cues.
- **Dogs that chew slippers** can carry them instead, so teach your dog to fetch! (See pages 166–167.)
- **Dogs need daily chewage**, so give rubber toys, natural hide chews, and food-based puzzle feeders. Puppies teethe between 8 and 25 weeks, and chewing helps relieve pain as adult teeth emerge: try frozen carrots to numb sore gums.

66

Consider it a compliment if your dog chews only your stuff—it means you're their favorite person.

99

SURVIVAL GUIDE

SURVIVAL GUIDE

Welcoming guests

Doorbells, buzzers, and knocks mean one thing to your dog—stranger danger! Whether you have a social butterfly or a nervous Nellie, without training, your dog is bound to hound visitors.

1

Train proactively

Why wait for visitors? When there's nobody at the door, use treats to train your dog first to go to their bed, then to sit and wait there. Then test your training: can you ask your dog to sit and wait while you answer the door and say "Hello!" to an imaginary guest or delivery person?

2

Be safety conscious

Don't answer the door while holding onto your dog. Instead, praise them when there's a ring or knock, even if they bark, then put them in another room or behind a baby gate with a chew to show that good things happen when someone is at the door and to keep guests safe.

3

Teach politeness

Once your dog has calmed down, show them how to approach and greet your guests. Invite the dog to say "Hi" by sitting in return for a treat. For shy or nervous dogs, have a relaxation mat in the room where you and your guests are, and send the dog there.

4

Prepare a safe space

Give your dog somewhere quiet they can escape to, like a crate or your bedroom, if they've had enough of your guests. We all know people who outstay their welcome!

5

Offer alternatives

Providing your dog with their favorite stuffed toy or a raw bone can be a great distraction from the initial excitement of greeting all of these new faces.

CHAPTER THREE

My amazing dog and other animals

Every interaction with another dog, a cat, or any other animal can give us insights into a dog's personality, confidence, and worries. By understanding how our dogs relate to other animals, we can help them all live more happily.

My dog hassles my cat

I've been a happy cat owner for years, but it all changed when I brought my dog home. She won't leave the cat alone, and now I'm worried the cat will move out!

the function?

Your dog wants to know if the cat is a friend, a foe, or a fun toy! Reading their body language before and after their interactions is crucial.

High tail says, "I'm wound up!"

Gentle panting, more friendly than a closed mouth

Bowing position: "Your move, cat!"

What's my dog thinking?

In part, this depends on your dog's personality. The fact is, cats and dogs have always had beef. Dogs bounce around and instinctively chase things that run, and cats are highly territorial. So your dog may see your cat as prey, a playmate, a catburglar, or a predator that could hurt her. Stay positive though. Cats and dogs can live in purrfect harmony if you introduce them slowly, give them their own space, and take their unique personality traits into account.

"Airplane" ears guard personal space

Arched back says, "Back off, I'm massive!"

What should I do?

In the moment:

- **When your dog** sees the cat, ask her to sit and give her a treat, so she understands that fun things happen when the cat appears.
- **Don't scold dogs for chasing**, as this can heighten their arousal and make things worse. If your dog is overexcited, take her out of the room to calm down.

In the long term:

- **Give cats and dogs** separate territories and use baby gates to keep dogs from chasing. Provide high spaces for cats so they can escape.
- **Cats are just as easy to train** as dogs! Use treats to teach both pets to sit on their beds when they're around each other to get them used to sharing a room.

Is your cat bullying?

Confident cats are great at using strong posture and quick bops to the face to set boundaries for cheeky pups, but an anxious cat's fierce or frightened reactions may teach a dog to chase, bite, and fight. Cats can also tease and bully dogs they feel have muscled in on "their" turf, so make sure you praise each pet for their patience and share your love—and your lap space—equally!

My dog chases anything that moves

My dog is 100 percent a good boy, except when he spots something fun to chase. It started with squirrels and cats; now it's joggers and even kids on bikes. He takes off and just ignores me calling.

the function?

Chasing is a survival instinct dogs use to work out the nature of something new. If the new thing reacts by running away, it's either a potential threat or prey.

Low tail to streamline body

Greyhound feet cross over, creating exceptional speed

What's my dog thinking?

Don't take it personally. Dogs instinctively chase things that move, and this behavior is often a reflex rather than a decision. Chase is a part of the "prey sequence" (see pages 104–105), and it is practically impossible to interrupt. Running produces the feel-good hormones dopamine and serotonin in both dogs and people. Add a shot of adrenaline into the mix from the thrill of chasing something, and you have a powerful and heady cocktail!

Super vision

Dogs are hypersensitive to movement and can spot an object moving hundreds of feet (meters) away. They have a field of vision of 240 degrees compared to our 200—so if you're standing directly behind them doing jumping jacks, they can see you! Dogs with a long nose have different depth perception and can see things in the distance better than flatter-faced dogs.

Lowered head to streamline for speed

Dilated pupils, as body is full of adrenaline

Mouth open, panting to bring oxygen to muscles

What should I do?

Be proactive! Start reward-based training around small animals, kids, and balls at puppy age. Join a training class and practice "watch me," "wait," "take" (a toy), and "leave it" cues.

Test your training outdoors, attaching a 32-foot (10-meter) training lead to your dog for safety:
- **Call your dog** and treat him for turning to his name.
- **Move closer**. If your dog stops and stares at something, throw treats down to break the stare. If he doesn't eat them, create distance and start again.
  - **Let the dog** look around. Praise, wait … then if he turns to look at you, treat him with food or a toy.

Work *with* your dog's instinct. Stop him from chasing bikes and joggers by teaching him to chase toys—or you!

"

A dog enjoying the thrill of the chase is almost impossible to call back, so training must target the moments before he starts to run.

"

ADVANCED DOGWATCHING

The prey sequence

Chasing is just one of the "prey sequence" behaviors. While most dogs move through each stage, some have been bred to specialize in a particular aspect (pages 14–15). Understanding this sequence is a great way to learn about your dog's unique breed traits, so you can train cues like "Wait" and "Watch me" during stages 1–3.

1 Scan

All dogs will look around, sniffing the air and panting gently, or "window shopping."

2 Eye/Freeze

The dog has spotted something, and their look turns to an icy stare. They are still, holding their breath and leaning forward, with ears pointing forward and tail high. Adrenaline pumps; it's decision time. This is specialist behavior for Guarding breeds, who need to know whether something is dinner or an uninvited guest. You may also see it in action when your dog eyeballs another dog while walking on the lead.

Specialists include: German Shepherds

3 Point/Stalk

Time for the sneak attack. Slow-moving, straight-backed, stealthy stalking with raised paws stops twigs from breaking underfoot and alerting the target. It also silently signals to the dog's pals that the hunt is on. Stalking is the trademark move of super-smart Collies, while the Pointer group is named for their specialist talent.

Specialists include: Pointers

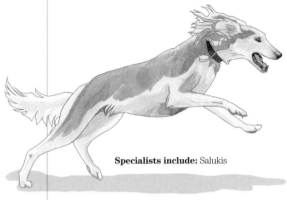

4 Chase

We're off! It's time for full-speed, every-second-counts pursuit. The dog's keen eyes study each twist and turn of their prey, anticipating its next move and cutting corners if necessary. Dogs are crafty, and a pair will quickly learn to route the prey together. All Hounds are especially thrilled by the chase.

Specialists include: Salukis

5 Bite

They who dare, bite! The dog must carefully select the safest place to clamp down and stop the prey in its tracks. Not all dogs are prone to deliver the bite, but many breeds use this stage in different ways: Mastiffs' strong jaws are perfect for pinning, Dachshunds offer lots of little bites and nip ankles, and some Gundogs can't help but greet you with slipper "prey" in their mouth (pp.84–85).

Specialists include: Dachshunds

6 Kill

It's game over. A specialist department of the Terrier gene pool, a prolonged squeeze on the neck to strangle prey or a swift shake to break its neck makes this as pain-free as possible and gets dinner on the table in no time. See this behavior when your dog captures certain toys: all squeakers must die (pp.166–167)!

Specialists include: Cairn Terriers

My dog uses other animals as furniture

I can't help laughing when my older dog uses my younger dog like a chair. One minute they're playing, the next she's sitting on him. She's done it to our playful kitten, too.

What's my dog thinking?

Your dog isn't being a jerk; this is dog language for "Shush! Stop it, you're making my head hurt." Dogs will sit on other dogs, cats, and even kids who are genuinely stressing them out— maybe by playing too boisterously or pestering them to play. Sitting on the other dog is a far better solution than resorting to aggression, as it brings a calm end to the situation. Nervous dogs will also sit on the shoulders of both human and dog friends to seek comfort and a sense of control if something is making them feel afraid.

What should I do?

In the moment:

- **Try not to laugh**, as this can encourage the "sitter" and make the other dog feel sad. It's best not to let things reach this point.
- **Call both parties** to separate living areas and encourage them to relax and enjoy their own space. Finding a treat you've already put there will help them learn to walk away.

In the long term:

- **Manage interactions** between your dog and whoever she tends to sit on. If anyone starts getting overexcited, give them some alternative entertainment before they drive her toward butt-to-face disciplinary measures. Keeping watch also stops frustrations building, and sat-upon individuals objecting with aggression.
- **Set clear boundaries** for play and other interactions at home, and make sure pets are getting the exercise and nutrition they need to relax properly.

> **❝**
>
> Sitting on other animals is your dog's alternative to shutting a door in their face. This isn't body language that we should copy!
>
> **❞**

Seeking comfort

Most dogs love sleeping together, and cuddling to share warmth is normal behavior, as they're born into large litters. A new puppy or rescue dog will often sit or lie down touching your first dog to recreate this comfort. If your first dog keeps moving away, then getting followed, step in before resentment builds. Help the needy dog gain enough confidence to sleep independently, with training and patience.

Clenched jaw and ears back: "I'm not impressed"

Sitting on another dog says, "We're done. Calm down now"

Sitting and facing away are calming signals to say, "No" and "Relax"

the function?

This dog body language for "Game over" is used as a time-out in extreme situations to enforce calmer behavior without using aggression.

Lying down with head down: "I give up"

SURVIVAL GUIDE

At the park

A trip to the park can be great for stretching your dog's legs, testing out your training, and socializing with friends and family. These top tips will ensure you both enjoy it every time.

1

Bring incentives

The park is a fun but highly distracting environment full of different sounds, smells, and creatures big and small. Bring toys and treats so you can center your dog's attention on you, especially once they're off the lead. Be prepared with poop bags, too!

2

Give your dog space

The swings or café might be your favorite spot, but your dog is more likely to love the bushes, woods, and tufts of pee-covered grass. Allow them plenty of sniffing time to make sure you both get some of what you enjoy most at the park.

3

Work on your recall

Your local park is a great place for puppy socialization and for training your dog. It's important when you're first visiting to keep your dog on a loose lead or a dropped long training line until their recall is reliable around children and other dogs and dangers like cars, cyclists, and ponds. Be aware that your dog might feel vulnerable on the lead around off-lead dogs, as their movement is restricted. Give them the space or loose lead they need to have relaxed dog "chats."

4

Teach manners

Use treats to train your dog to ask and wait for your okay before bounding up to greet or play with other dogs. Some dogs, both on and off the lead, can get grumpy or aggressive if they're approached without warning or permission.

109

My dog hates other dogs

I took my dog to training classes, socialized him with friends' dogs, and got him neutered at 6 months, so why does he still hate other dogs? He either avoids them or growls and snaps.

the function?

Examine what your dog gains by this behavior (see pages 22-23). Perhaps you walk away with him or stop offering other dogs treats?

What's my dog thinking?

The social arena can be just as daunting for a dog as the playground was for you. Dogs have personality clashes, and some are naturally shy. But if your dog avoids or shows aggression toward every other dog, he's probably guarding his personal space, his stuff, or you out of fear. This could be due to a previous experience in the litter, training class, or daycare that wasn't safe or fun for him. Over time, this socially stressed dog learns to growl, snap, and even bite if his less aggressive signals to other dogs get ignored (see pages 150–151).

What should I do?

In the moment:

Praise and treat your dog whenever he spots another dog, then turn and walk away. He'll learn that seeing other dogs is positive, and he doesn't need to use aggression to earn space from them.

In the long term:

- **Arrange lead walks** with a placid dog, with help from a qualified behaviorist who uses positive training techniques. Keep the dogs parallel and a

66

Be your dog's safe space in social situations so he can escape without learning to use aggression.

99

Young or playful dogs can be overwhelming

reasonable distance apart so your dog can focus on you and eat treats. Gradually reduce the distance and build in some relaxed greetings.

- **Socialize with calm** adult dogs that offer reassuring behaviors like sniffing, walking away, and gentle play rather than bouncy young dogs that could antagonize yours.
- **Don't hang out with dogs** if you don't need to! Some dogs are happy to live life without dog friends.

Antisocial experiences

All kinds of badly managed group situations can inflict lasting trauma on a dog. For example, not regulating overly boisterous play while socializing with friends who have dogs, spending time in noisy boarding kennels, a dog park with a bullying dog in it, or even living with another dog that quietly bullies without us realizing it can all make a sociable dog become aggressive toward other dogs.

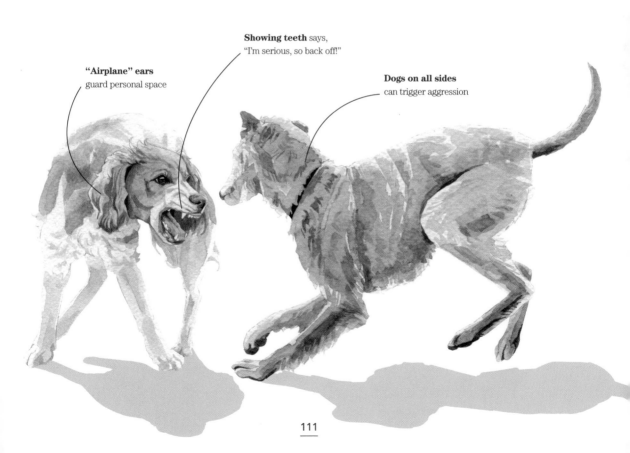

"Airplane" ears guard personal space

Showing teeth says, "I'm serious, so back off!"

Dogs on all sides can trigger aggression

Other dogs hate my dog

No matter how often I try, when I introduce my dog to other dogs, they reject my poor girl. We've had growling, snapping, and even full-blown attacks. Why do they all hate her so much?

What's my dog thinking?

Your dog is probably just as confused as you about why she's getting shunned. She may be naturally shy, which could cause some dogs to bully her. Dogs can smell the stress hormone cortisol, and this can lead to aggression and fights breaking out, seemingly from nowhere. Or she may get told off because she's approaching other dogs too fast, too playfully, or being rude to their human. You will need to practice spotting body language signals—including other dogs' postures and their tail positions—to really understand what your dog is thinking and help her relax and offer a friendly "handshake" (see pages 114–115).

> **66**
>
> Dogs that get repeatedly attacked are likely to learn defensive aggression and need professional support from a qualified behaviorist using force-free techniques.
>
> **99**

Whites of eyes: either fearful or guarding space

Ears back in a posture of retreat

Covered teeth says, "I mean no harm"

Off-balance posture: shock and uncertainty where to turn

What should I do?

In the moment:

Take your dog out of the situation; if she has already scrapped with another dog, they're unlikely to become friends. Leaving dogs to work it out between themselves will let your dog either learn to bully or get bullied in the future.

In the long term:

- **Teach loose-lead walking** (see pages 170–171) and "Watch me" without other dogs around. Then practice with them at a distance before moving closer, so your dog doesn't pull toward others or stare.
- **Play scentwork games** and teach sniffing by throwing treats to help your dog relax and show other dogs she's calm and under control.
- **Be super fun** when other dogs are around! Giving your dog a different focus by getting her to play tug or fetch games with you will relax her.
- **Film interactions** with other dogs to help identify their subtle body language clues.

Dogs on leads may feel trapped, increasing their reactivity

Teeth on show says, "Heck no!"

Tail high and alert with adrenaline

Forward posture and ears say, "I mean it!"

Sniffing trouble?

Although we know that dogs' scent marking is a complex "conversation" and not simply territorial graffiti, we still know little about their world of scent (see pages 12–13). One theory is that dogs meet each other many times in the world of smell and argue repeatedly on pee "forums," well before the day they actually meet head to head in a fight.

The dog handshake

Just as our ancestors shook hands to prove they weren't armed, dogs offer each other gestures of goodwill when they meet. A dog's weapons are in its mouth, so trusting a new friend is vital before letting them anywhere near your delicate stomach or crown jewels! Some greetings are less than perfect (see pages 116–119), but here's how an ideal dog "handshake" should go.

1 Face sniff

First dates and interviews are both scary and exciting, and such encounters are no less intimidating for dogs. Face sniffing allows both dogs to check subtle signs of calmness and confidence or tension in the other dog's eyes, face, and mouth before permitting a full body check. They also get valuable scent information from salivary glands in the lips; you may see some gentle mouth licking as an appeasement gesture to keep things friendly.

2 Head turn

Giving a subtle head turn, with soft eyes and a relaxed body posture, is Dog for "Carry on," and it gives the other dog permission to sniff the rest of the body. Some dogs will first spend some time sniffing the auricular glands near the ears.

3 Urogenital sniffing

By scenting the undercarriage and stomach, each dog collects pheromone information from the other's urogenital system (pp.12-13). A dog being sniffed may lift their leg to give the other dog better access. Licking this area is normal, too—even if it's embarrassing for us. If one dog walks off and the other tries to keep licking, it's best to separate them.

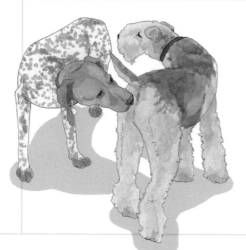

4 Butt sniff and circle

This is the classic end of a good dog handshake—and maybe the start of a great play session. Butt sniffing collects information from the anal glands about the other dog's age, sex, reproductive status, health, stress level, and more. As both dogs lean in to sniff, they can end up going around in circles. If they're on leads, follow them; getting tangled may accidentally encourage aggression.

When my dog meets another dog ...

... I never really know what's going to happen. I've seen him bark, roll over, and even strut in like he's the "big dog." I wonder if he'll ever make friends?

What's my dog thinking?

It depends. Every dog meeting is unique and is affected by the age, sex, breed, personality, and previous experiences of *both* dogs. When your dog first sees another dog, he may bow (pp.80–81) or try any of the "hello" behaviors shown here—or others. Each action is a "play" to see what the other dog will do next; dog conversations are fluid and change constantly in response to posture, motivation, and mood. Your dog may roll submissively at first, then if the other dog is too intense, instantly switch tactics and air snap.

"Hello" ... now what?

Once they're up close, socializing is as complex for dogs as it is for us. They need repeated experiences to learn how to offer a polite "handshake" (pp.114–115). Meanwhile, a certain greeting style could make your dog feel safer or more in control—you may see impolite plays like humping (pp.62–63) or others shown here.

Friendly to "floozie"

Head low and body wiggling, a gentle wobble gives your dog the best chance of making friends, with its nonthreatening, easy manner. But if he's too submissive and flings himself onto his back to say hello, this "floozie" play can easily annoy other dogs.

What should I do?

Trust a friendly wobbler to manage most situations, but practice recall around other dogs, in case your dog becomes a friendly space invader (see opposite). If he's a bit of a floozie, try socializing with calm older dogs and plenty of recall practice.

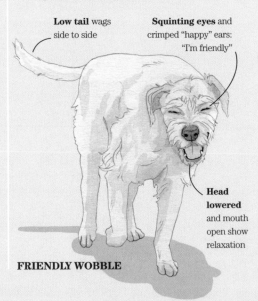

Low tail wags side to side

Squinting eyes and crimped "happy" ears: "I'm friendly"

Head lowered and mouth open show relaxation

FRIENDLY WOBBLE

Barking

Shouting isn't necessary to make friends; if your dog often barks on approach, he's probably saying "Hey!" or "Back off!" because he feels threatened or unsure.

What should I do?

Praise and treat your dog whenever he sees other dogs at a distance, and change direction sometimes to show him he doesn't have to say hello. Practice gradually walking closer to other dogs while giving your dog treats, then walk away again.

Stalking

Most dogs stop a fair distance away, then approach in stages to gather scent information and assess friendliness. But some drop low into a sneaky stalk before bounding forward in ambush mode. This is a breed trait of Herding dogs, but it can be a sign of anxiety in others.

the function?

Ultimately, every dog meeting is an attempt to build community. Like us, dogs just want to be safe, avoid conflict, make friends, and find a mate.

What should I do?

Approach dogs from the side, not head on, to soften your dog's intensity; reward looking back at you; and practice recall.

Space invading

Dogs that haven't learned to ask for greetings may bolt at others without warning to intimidate them into play; this "hello" can cause serious trouble with nervous dogs. Alternatively, if your dog pumps his chest or swaggers over, he's probably pretending to be more confident than he feels; he may go on to lean his neck over or put paws onto other dogs to gain height.

What should I do?

Socialize space invaders with older dogs to slow them down and help them learn politeness. If another dog rushes at yours, calmly walk away or tell the owner your dog doesn't want to play. Parallel walking with other dogs lets height seekers learn more relaxed ways to make new friends, like sniffing and head turns.

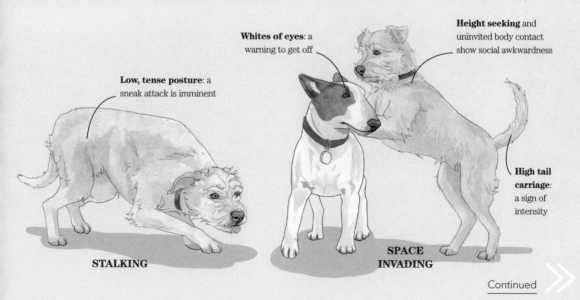

Low, tense posture: a sneak attack is imminent

Whites of eyes: a warning to get off

Height seeking and uninvited body contact show social awkwardness

High tail carriage: a sign of intensity

STALKING

SPACE INVADING

Continued

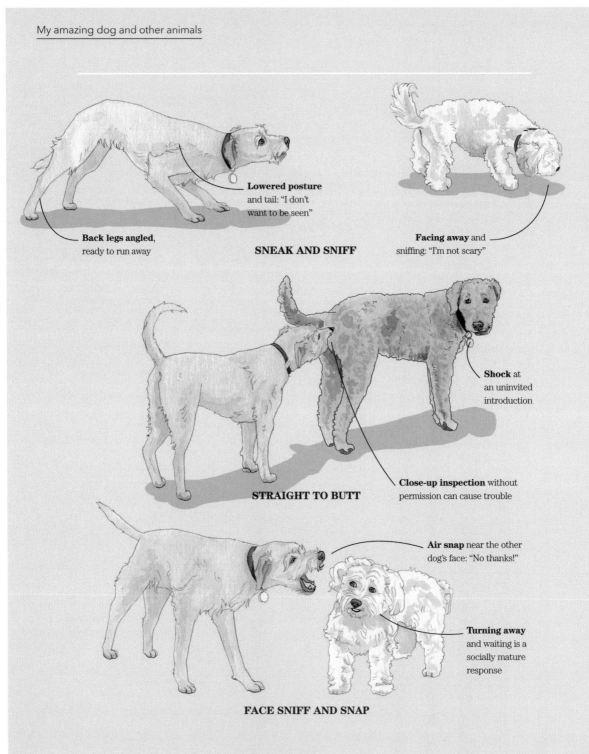

Lowered posture and tail: "I don't want to be seen"

Back legs angled, ready to run away

SNEAK AND SNIFF

Facing away and sniffing: "I'm not scary"

Shock at an uninvited introduction

Close-up inspection without permission can cause trouble

STRAIGHT TO BUTT

Air snap near the other dog's face: "No thanks!"

Turning away and waiting is a socially mature response

FACE SNIFF AND SNAP

Sneak and sniff

Anxious dogs often want to sniff others without being sniffed in return. Your dog will shift around in circles, sit down, or retreat in order to guard his own butt—then run up and sniff another dog's when they're not looking.

What should I do?

Give your sneaky sniffer plenty of space to approach other dogs and retreat if he needs to, by using either a loose lead or no lead, and calmly protect him from mixing with space invaders. He'll gain confidence with time and a consistent, chilled social group.

Straight to butt

Going straight in for a butt close-up without first checking for permission at the other dog's face is a rude way to begin a conversation! Your pushy butt sniffer hasn't learned that yet, but expect him to be told off by other dogs for his lack of social etiquette.

What should I do?

Help your cheeky Charlie relax by praising him when he notices other dogs in the distance. When you get close, throw treats down to teach him to offer calming ground sniffs, and walk in parallel with another dog before greeting them.

Face sniff ... and snap

The face sniff is the first step in the ideal dog handshake (pp.114–115). But sometimes one dog may eyeball the other and hold an intense stare for too long, curl a lip, or even snap the air as a warning (pp.154–155). This often happens when two dogs greet each other on leads—it means butts aren't getting sniffed today!

What should I do?

Avoid greeting other dogs that are also on leads, treat your dog whenever he sees another dog to show him this is a good thing, and practice recall. If another dog air snaps, walk yours away— regaining space and teaching him that you can protect him will help him calm down. When you meet a dog, keep your dog's lead loose, as lead tension can create aggression (pp.170–171).

Ghosting

Your dog may pretend another dog doesn't exist, or even walk away on seeing them. "Ghosting" or oblivious dogs are either confident and aloof adults or very socially anxious and desperate to avoid meetings; watch your dog's body language signals for clues.

What should I do?

To create positive associations, treat your dog when you spot another dog in the distance and retreat with him when he wants to leave.

GHOSTING

Looking up to watch for space invaders

Sniffing helps him look busy

Not all dogs need dog friends to be happy, but a dog that offers polite greetings to other dogs is a joy for the whole community.

What is fair play?

Wanna play? Even as adults, many dog breeds play with a puppylike charm that's joyful to watch. Play isn't just fun, it's functional, too; dogs use it to practice flirting, fighting, hunting, or just make friends by swapping scent. Genuine play has to be fun for both dogs, so when you spot these signs, you'll know it's game on! (For red flags that it's no longer fun, see pages 122–123.)

Play bows

Every great game starts with an invitation. A fair player invites play by bowing, and if the other dog wants to accept, they bow back.

No eyeballing

Dogs generally avoid head-to-head confrontations during play. They'll stay side on to each other, or in a T-shape.

Faking it

Great play has exaggerated soft, bouncy movements and lots of noise. Everything about it tells the other dog, "I'm only playing!" It should look like Capoeira, the beautiful martial art of mirroring a partner, with fake bites and very little real body contact.

Time-outs

Great play can get physical, but fair players keep their playmate happy by allowing them to hit pause. One dog may ask for a time-out by sitting, lying down, or walking off to do some sniffing.

Shake off

Both dogs shaking their whole body during and after a play bout is a sign that they are managing excitement and staying relaxed. The "shake off" is like a deep breath out; it tells us they have let go of anything that has just happened.

Self-handicapping

In fair play, dogs will "self-handicap" to build trust with a play partner—like a parent letting their toddler "win." Rolling or falling over invites a playmate back into the game if they have taken a break, and also helps if one dog is getting overexcited.

Swapsies

Play is a conversation, not a monologue, and must be equal to be enjoyed. Dogs should swap roles, so the chaser becomes the chased, and the dog on top takes a turn underneath.

Keep it fair

If you're not sure play is still fair, separate the dogs for 20 seconds and give them something else to do, like playing "find it" with treats. If one dog takes the chance to walk away, they needed a break. Great dogwatching!

ADVANCED DOGWATCHING

What is unfair play?

Red card! Just as school playgrounds need an adult pair of eyes to ensure kids don't turn savage, dog playtime needs refereeing because things can quickly turn nasty. Whenever you see moves like not asking for permission or disrespecting personal space, calmly interrupt and help both dogs take a break.

Pinning ... with teeth

Fair play has fake biting and hardly any body contact (see pages 120–121), but some dogs love chasing and pinning others down and may bite hard on legs, necks, and ears. These "sharks" are often teenagers; their patient playmates get used as punching bags, teaching them it's okay to use teeth. If either dog has teeth on show, the "game" has turned sour.

Referee! Protect the pinned or bitten dog and provide more structured play, ideally using toys, before the punky pup becomes a proper thug.

Can't catch me!

Dogs playing fair chase games should swap roles, so one-sided chasing is a red flag. Socially mature dogs will sometimes use running as a strategy to tire out a playmate they're finding too strong or a little rude.

Referee! Catch or distract the chaser, if the race doesn't stop naturally— or the chased dog could panic and bolt.

The "hug"

"Look, they're hugging!" No, they're not. Standing face to face and grappling is the dog equivalent of thumb wrestling and will only escalate into unpleasantness. It starts with some height seeking to establish who's tallest, but left unchecked, this "play" can teach socially awkward dogs to enjoy bullying or expect to wrestle every dog they meet, making them anxious or aggressive.

Referee! Walk these dogs together on loose leads so they can make friends by "mirroring" instead.

Best of 100?

Nice play bouts happen for 5-10 minutes and stop naturally, as one dog walks off to sniff or lie down. Dogs that want to play all day long aren't playing— they're battling. The moment another dog stops or "wins" a play fight, this frustrated dog wants to start again.

Referee! Help them settle for best of three by showing them alternative games like tug of war on toys or "find it" using treats to encourage sniffing.

Mobbing

Although dogs can play perfectly well in larger groups, sometimes they will gang up on each other. Teaming up with your friends to manipulate the space of another dog by cornering or "mobbing" them isn't playful or friendly.

Referee! Walk calmly between the dogs to break their focus and help the cornered dog escape to safety.

My dog rolls in animal poop—and worse!

Why is "eau d'animal" my dog's favorite perfume? Doesn't matter if it's fox poop, a dead badger, or worse—she will find it and roll in it!

What's my dog thinking?

Everyone loves dressing up, and for your dog, who "sees" the world through her nose, rolling in gross things is the equivalent of putting on an animal costume. An ancient and natural hunting instinct, rolling in feces or dead animals covers dogs in the smell of their prey, helping them blend in and sneak up on whatever they're stalking. Doing this also leaves the smell of your dog behind, so other dogs who arrive later can identify that she's already seen and claimed this disgusting "treasure."

Story in scent

Rolling in revolting stuff also performs a secondary storytelling function. Unlike honey bees, which waggle to tell the hive they've found honey, dogs don't relate their hunting journey through expressive dance. Instead, they collect a smear of their experience along their shoulder to take home, so the rest of the pack can "read" their hunting story through smell.

What should I do?

In the moment:

Luckily, dogs warn us they're about to roll by running off enthusiastically and taking a good long sniff of their target perfume. Using the "leave it" and "come" cues when you spot your dog bouncing off can help curb this filthy habit.

In the long term:

- **Don't keep bathing** your dog in perfumed shampoos that smell nice to us. These are overwhelming to your dog's super-sensitive nose and may prompt her to go hunting for a more dog-oriented hair product.
- **Create alternatives** for dogs that enjoy hunting, like redirecting them to play games with you using a flirt pole (which has an attached rope and toy). You can also sign up for scentwork or trailing classes and put that fantastic nose to good use.

the function?

Rolling creates camouflage for dogs and leaves a scent stamp so other dogs can spot their hunting movements.

Neck and shoulder scent glands rubbing on the "treasure"

> 66
>
> Rolling in poop and remains is instinctive behavior and is almost impossible to stop—even with the threat of a bath!
>
> 99

Paws bracing, ready to roll over

Open mouth to get a full hit of the bouquet

My dog barks at the mail carrier

My dog hates mail carriers! He waits for deliveries every day and charges to the door to defend his turf. It used to be funny, until he ripped up a really important letter.

What's my dog thinking?

The problem with mail carriers is they never come in. Friends are invited into the home, so your dog can easily distinguish them, whereas deliveries are tantamount to attempted burglary. From your dog's perspective, the same unknown, sneaky human approaches his own human's den every day and tries to get in. They fail and go away again *because* he barks and charges after them—but not before dropping off a "bomb" that any decent guard dog must instantly destroy! Mail shredding is frustrating, but attacking the mail carrier could land your pet in dog jail, so time to get training.

> 66
>
> Your dog will be naturally suspicious of anyone or anything approaching and retreating from the front door.
>
> 99

Maildog training

It might seem impossible, but dogs that destroy mail can be trained to fetch it using treat-based training. Start by teaching your dog to fetch toys (see pages 166–167). Then use old envelopes to teach your dog to "Take it" and "Bring it." Finally, push envelopes into the mailbox for your dog to remove gently and deliver to you. There's a good maildog!

Hackles up to look big and frighten the "attacker"

Head high and neck arched

Tail high and wagging, pumped for the "fight"

Barking, snarling, or panting

What should I do?

In the moment:

- **When the mail carrier** arrives, praise your dog with a "Thank you!", and call him over to his bed for a treat. Changing the pattern of your dog's behavior is crucial to curbing his enthusiasm.
- **Don't tell your dog off** for going crazy when the mail carrier arrives, or he'll see all mail carriers and delivery people as the source of your stress, which will make him hate them even more.

In the long term:

- **Protect your mail** as well as the mail carrier by using an outdoor mailbox or caging inside your entrance door to stop letters— or fingers—from getting chewed.
- **Teach your dog to sit** and wait on his bed while you walk to the front door and back to greet fake guests and accept fake mail. Establishing this protocol for every visitor and guest will help your dog succeed when it really counts.

the function?

Guarding your home from threats is valiant work, and ripping mail is a satisfying calming behavior that helps your dog unwind after the "battle."

My dog brings all the boys to the yard

My dog has been in heat before but never let a male near her. Now, whenever one approaches our fence or she meets one at the park, she's practically twerking!

What's my dog thinking?

There is only one diagnosis: you have a sexy girl. Unspayed female dogs come into "heat" twice a year from around 6 months old, and this "season" lasts between 2 and 4 weeks, depending on breed. A young female will usually reject the advances of a pushy Romeo who doesn't first make the effort to woo her with neck nibbling and play. Over time though, she will become just as assertive herself with nearby males while she's at peak fertility. So if you see her presenting her bottom, get her out of the danger zone!

> 66
>
> Male dogs will smell a female dog in heat from miles away and will struggle with recall as long as there's a chance of mating with her.
>
> 99

What should I do?

Walk your dog on a lead and be careful where you exercise her. Male dogs will find her and follow her for miles, so choose a safe space to exercise her for a few weeks.

Keep your dog away from carpets and upholstery while she's spotting blood, but be sure to give her a comfy space to eat dog ice cream and watch romcoms!

If you also live with a male dog that isn't neutered and you aren't trying to breed puppies, separate the dogs as soon as you notice signs your female is coming into heat.

Managing a female in heat can be complex; once your dog has reached full maturity, at around 18–24 months, consider getting her spayed.

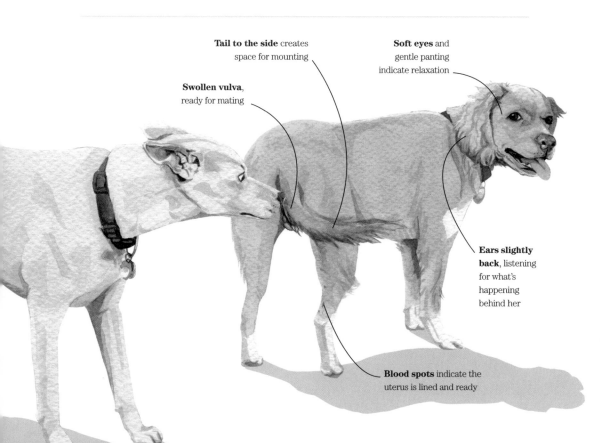

Tail to the side creates space for mounting

Soft eyes and gentle panting indicate relaxation

Swollen vulva, ready for mating

Ears slightly back, listening for what's happening behind her

Blood spots indicate the uterus is lined and ready

the function?

Standing with her tail to one side is the easiest way for your girl to say, "Hey you! I'm fertile and ready to be mated."

Signs your dog's in heat

Unlike humans, female dogs are ready to mate when their period starts. Signs your female dog is in heat include excessive licking of her rear end; a visibly swollen vulva followed by small blood spots in the area; and behavioral changes like clinginess, restlessness, lack of appetite, nervousness, more frequent urination, and occasionally aggression. That's right—our dogs get PMS as well!

SURVIVAL GUIDE

Visiting dog friends

*Friends are the family we choose … unless you're a dog, and
your owner's friends have dogs you're forced to hang out with.
The good news is that it's easy to make socializing fun and fair.*

1
Walk them first
It's best to let the dogs meet on neutral ground on a walk together so you can check they'll get along. Then let them enter your friend's home at the same time to stop the resident dog from feeling too territorial.

2
Open doors
Create as much room as possible for the dogs to run around indoors and get used to each other when you get to your friend's place. Play "find it" by throwing treats for both dogs to get them sniffing together sociably.

3
Where shall I sit?
Take your dog's bed or mat when you go to your friends' houses to give your dog their own seat in this new and strange-smelling place and to discourage your dog from stealing the resident dog's bed.

4
Guests bring prizes
Get the treats out and make sure you give both dogs delicious rewards for relaxing calmly in their own beds. Then they'll both look forward to your next visit, too!

5
Set house rules
Decide on some boundaries with your friends. Resident dogs will tell other dogs off if they cross a line, so keep the peace by helping your dog stick to the house rules.

6
Time apart
Make sure there is space for the dogs to have some time away from each other, if they need it to sleep or just to chill out alone with a calming chew.

CHAPTER FOUR

What is *up* with my amazing dog?

Sometimes our dogs do things that worry or upset us. It's important to put strange or unusual behavior into its full context, so you can properly understand why your dog is acting this way and respond appropriately and positively.

My dog won't eat

I feed my dog before work, but when I come back, nothing is gone.
It's the best food I can buy, so why won't she eat it?

What's my dog thinking?

One of the first signs a dog isn't feeling well is lack of appetite (see pages 136–137), but there are many possible reasons for not eating. For example, your dog may see a link between being fed and you leaving, which puts her off breakfast. She may not like the food or could be bored with the taste; like children, some dogs are smart enough to wait and see if something better gets offered when they don't eat. Watch carefully; does your dog sniff food and walk away, try some and spit it out, or avoid it altogether?

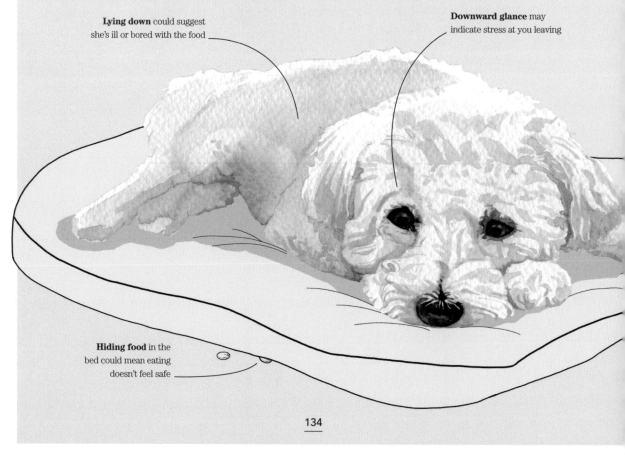

Lying down could suggest she's ill or bored with the food

Downward glance may indicate stress at you leaving

Hiding food in the bed could mean eating doesn't feel safe

Fight-or-flight response

We may think a dog isn't treat-oriented, but there could be another reason for ignoring snacks. Running from danger is a higher priority, and the fight-or-flight response shuts down the dog's digestive system as blood travels to the legs, away from the stomach. If a dog is worried while walking, in the car, or at home, the first obvious sign is a head turn away from even the most delectable treat.

the function?

Your dog isn't eating, as eating isn't a priority. Look at the context, apply the "What's the function?" formula (see pages 22–23), then seek a vet's advice.

What should I do?

In the moment:

Relax. Pushing the bowl, frowning, or stressing at your dog is likely to put her off eating even more.

In the long term:

- **Exercise your dog first**. Some dogs won't eat breakfast until they've worked up an appetite.
- **Make your dog earn it!** Present all food lovingly, like it's a prize roast dinner, and ask her to sit and wait before giving the okay to eat.
- **Try alternative presentation**, like food-based toys that roll, or tossing pieces of food in the yard for a fun game of "find it."
- **Vary dog food flavors**, or consider switching to a raw or fresh diet that's highly palatable and low in preservatives.
- **If your dog still isn't eating** even high-value treats after 24 hours, consult your vet.

Spitting out food could indicate it isn't tasty, or hurts teeth

If you own a Labrador and this page is *still* relevant to you, call the vet immediately!

ADVANCED DOGWATCHING

Signs of illness

Our dogs are mostly honest about how they feel, except when they're not well; hiding pain was necessary for ancestors in the wild, where a sick dog was a burden on the pack. Obvious signs of illness include loss of appetite, vomiting, and diarrhea, but when the clue is in your dog's behavior, it can be easier to overlook. These are some potential signals.

Scooting

This behavior looks like your dog is wiping their butt. The most likely cause is blocked anal glands that are sore and need to be expressed by a vet (see pages 12–13). The good news is that it's not life threatening; the bad news is the smell! But ignoring this could lead to infection and an abscess.

Nose rubbing and paw or leg chewing

Itchy noses, paws, and skin are usually signs of an allergic reaction. Inhaling grass pollen and dust mites can trigger allergies; if the dog rubs their nose and chews their paws at around the same time of day, it's often food related. Be aware: dogs may also leg chew as a way to cope with a more complex internal discomfort that they can't reach.

Hang dog

Sometimes the signs are really subtle, like restlessness; oversleeping; or just a "hang dog" posture with dilated pupils, bunched fur, a tense stomach, and panting. Dogs often bear discomfort without whining, so even if they're only acting a little strangely, it's still cause for a vet visit.

Unusual aggression

If your normally chill dog suddenly becomes grumpy or growls or snaps at you for no obvious reason, get to the vet. Pain from illness or an injury is a likely trigger; this could be anything from a sore tooth or ear infection to, sadly, cancer.

Nesting

You might be surprised to see your dog burrow into her bedding, protect a particular soft toy, seem depressed, and even lactate. These are symptoms of false pregnancy. Hormonal changes after each heat can convince an intact female she's having pups, so she should come out of this naturally—but consult your vet if it happens repeatedly.

Excessive surface licking

Does your dog keep licking an odd surface, like walls, furniture, your body, or even the air? This could indicate an underlying digestive health problem. One scientific research study of 19 dogs that did this daily found the majority had a gastrointestinal illness, such as pancreatitis or irritable bowel syndrome.

My dog eats poop

My dog is a greedy pottymouth who would eat all the poop he could get if I didn't stop him—the cat's, other dogs', and even his own. And yes, he does try to kiss me with that mouth!

What's my dog thinking?

Although poop eating is one of the main reasons dogs get abandoned, it is a natural behavior. Female dogs lick newborns to stimulate them to start pottying, then keep eating their poop to prevent predators from finding the litter. Sometimes adult dogs eat poop because they're worried about neighborhood threats and are trying to hide their smell. Depending on your reaction to this nasty habit, your dog may eat poop because he thinks it's valuable, or to get more of your attention (see pages 22–23). The cause might also be physical; for example, a dog with irritable bowel syndrome may not fully digest food and may enjoy eating it again.

> **66**
>
> Eating poop is gross, but it is instinctive for dogs, so keep calm and keep them away from temptation whenever possible.
>
> **99**

What should I do?

In the moment:

- **Don't shout** or punish your dog; this will make the behavior worse if it is stress related. Instead, practice teaching the "leave it" cue, using positive reinforcement training methods.
- **Praise and call your dog** indoors for a treat when he goes in the yard, then go straight back out and pick up the poop. A clean yard means fresher dog breath!

In the long term:

- **If your dog constantly searches** for "fast food" on walks, use a basket muzzle to reduce the chances of snacking success.
- **Book a blood test** with the vet to check your dog's digestive and liver functions and to make sure his worming treatments are up to date.
- **Don't waste money** on products designed to make poop taste bad to your dog: these won't deter a dedicated poop-aholic.

Rounded topline and tensed
stomach shows stress

Waste not, want not

Coprophagy (eating poop) is actually
seen in many animal species. Beavers,
rabbits, rodents, and elephants are
among the mammals that will eat
their own feces. Cat poop is
particularly tempting to dogs,
as cats need a higher protein
content in their food than
dogs, which makes their
poop extra meaty.

Eyes checking
for potential rivals

Ears alert, listening for disruptions

My dog eats toys

My dog swallows her toys whole. We've been to the vet so many times, I'm always on guard now. She steals and eats socks, towels, and the kids' toys, too, so they chase her to get them back.

What's my dog thinking?

Possession is nine-tenths of the law in Dogland, and some pups learn this behavior from their mother or littermates if they're born somewhere stressful, like a shelter. Sadly, many human puppy parents don't realize the damage they can do to the relationship by repeatedly removing items from their pup's mouth while it's exploring. The dog learns that the only way to keep things is to swallow them before they're taken away. This behavior is a sign that your dog is worried and needs help. If she's holding something, negotiate to get it back. Demanding she drops it, or snatching it, will reinforce swallowing.

Discomfort eating

Eating toys, socks, blankets, rocks, or other strange things is a symptom of something deeper that takes compassion and patience to fix. Some dogs develop Pica, a condition where they obsessively eat nonfood items, even if it makes them ill. It's often seen in Gundog breeds, which are bred to carry things in their mouths.

What should I do?

In the moment:

- **Try not to freak out** whenever your dog picks things up. You can stimulate swallowing if you suddenly launch yourself at the dog. And don't send the kids in to get things back.
- **Throw down treats** and use praise to help the dog drop or swap with you. If she's already avoiding you, leave the room and shut the door behind you. Count to five and reopen the door—most dogs will come out, leaving the item behind.
- **Small things like pebbles** are likely to pass through your dog. Observe her for 24 hours, and if you see any signs of sickness or difficulty going potty, call the vet. If you're worried, call immediately, as obstructions can be deadly.

In the long term:

Consult a qualified behaviorist who uses force-free techniques to find solutions to this complex behavior.

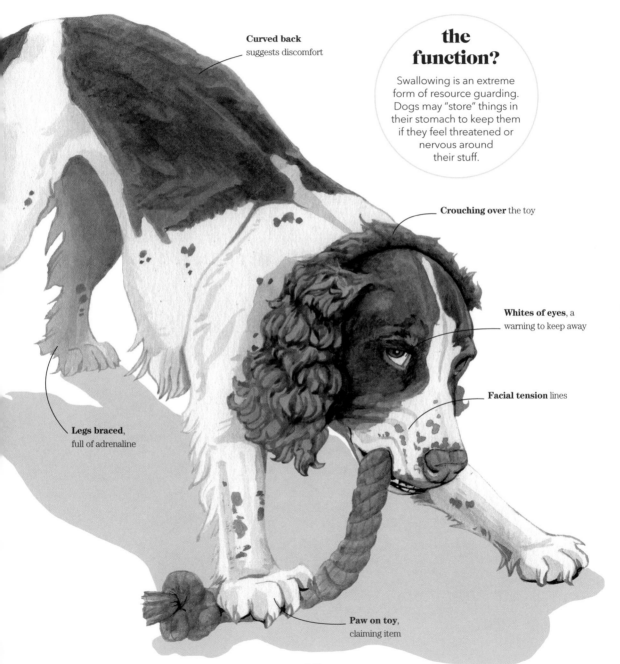

Curved back
suggests discomfort

the function?

Swallowing is an extreme form of resource guarding. Dogs may "store" things in their stomach to keep them if they feel threatened or nervous around their stuff.

Crouching over the toy

Whites of eyes, a warning to keep away

Facial tension lines

Legs braced, full of adrenaline

Paw on toy, claiming item

141

SURVIVAL GUIDE

Being around kids

It's vital for children to learn to make friends with dogs so they grow up safe and confident around them. Guidance and training are paramount to ensure kids and dogs respect each other's space.

1
Teach dogs to respect kids

Train your dog to sit before greeting children and to lie down on their bed or walk away if they're feeling uncomfortable using treats and praise. Although dogs recognize human "puppies" and are often naturally more gentle around them, jumping up, following, or sniffing little people's faces can be intimidating and create phobias early in life.

2
Teach kids to respect dogs

Teach children to ask owners if they can greet a dog and to let the dog smell their hand before any touching. It's best at any age to ask permission to touch, even if you know the dog. Kids also need to learn what a scared or stressed dog looks like, to stand still with arms crossed if a dog follows or chases them, and not to bombard on-lead dogs with attention.

3
Consider their age

Older children are more capable of understanding a dog's point of view and how to behave around them, whereas young children haven't fully developed the concept of "other," so telling them off for poking the dog is pointless. If your child is under 5, focus your training on the dog first.

4
Always supervise

Monitoring kids' behavior and dogs' body language is essential when they are together. Dogs will bite to say, "No!" if their whispers of discomfort haven't been heard by the adult in charge (pp.150–151). Very few parents can forgive a dog that bites a child, and the consequences can be fatal.

My dog pees indoors and on the furniture

I housetrained my dog, but he keeps peeing on the carpet and the couch. I've tried deterrent "keep away" sprays and a citronella collar, but he still pees when my back is turned. Is he just being naughty?

What's my dog thinking?

To dogs, pee isn't simply waste—it's expressive and communicative, too. Dogs will often urinate on a new bed once or twice to make it smell familiar, but if your dog is regularly peeing indoors and he's healthy, it's likely he's feeling stressed by something. This could be anything from a change in your daily schedule to kids arguing. He isn't marking his territory or trying to assert dominance over you though. While it's natural to feel frustrated with your little "pee-casso," try to step back and look for clues about what he's telling you (see pages 20–21).

What should I do?

In the moment:

Don't get angry. If the behavior is based on anxiety, this is likely to make your dog worse and encourage him to hide when he needs to go—making potty training tricky.

In the long term:

- **Take your dog to the vet**. He may have a urinary tract infection, an underlying health problem, or incontinence.
- **Restart housetraining**. Take your dog (or pup) outside every hour and pay him with a treat if he pees outside. Eventually, he'll save them up for outdoors.
- **Find ways to help your dog** feel more relaxed. A consistent routine, clear and loving boundaries, mentally enriching toys, and dopamine-based collars or diffusers will all support relaxation.
- **If your dog mostly pees** while you're out, revisit your separation routine (see pages 178–179).
- **Use biological detergent** to clean up urine. Dogs' super-sensitive noses often lead them to pee again in the same spot.

the function?

Urination can be accidental, unintentional, stress related or due to sickness. Zoom out and look at what's going on around your dog (see pages 22–23).

Watching for dangers, as he feels vulnerable while peeing

Whites of eyes showing means keep away

High, curled tail: a sign of arousal and tension

Mouth tension says, "I'm feeling stressed"

Height matters

Dogs use urine to communicate detailed information about themselves (pages 12–13). For males, and some females, cocking their leg lets them aim their pee signature as high as possible and get the best coverage on dog "news channels." Some dogs may even do an impressive handstand to pee, so they can be part of a "conversation" going on over their head!

145

My dog gets his willy out!

I thought I could already see my dog's penis, but apparently not. He saved this special red "surprise" for the day we visited my partner's family for lunch. Thanks, boy!

What's my dog thinking?

"Red rocket," "lipstick," or "crowning glory": whatever you call it, the sudden appearance of your dog's erect penis for no obvious reason will encourage some people—especially inquisitive children—to stop and, no pun intended, point it out. Dogs naturally get aroused, even if they're neutered, but it's not always the potential for sex that gets them going. So it definitely doesn't mean your dog fancies you! The anticipation of a walk, training session, or good meal can prompt a red-rocket response. Arousal can also be a sign that there is something making your dog anxious.

Erectile dysfunctions

Phimosis is the medical term for when the dog's penis struggles to get out of the prepuce. Sometimes the dog's penis doesn't go back inside it; then, *paraphimosis* is when a nonerect penis remains stuck outside, while *priapism* is when the erect penis can't get back home! And did you also know your dog's penis has a bone inside it? Fascinating ... sort of.

What should I do?

In the moment:

- **Try ignoring it** and hope that it goes away! Some trainers believe this is the best way to make sure you're not accidentally encouraging or rewarding this behavior.
- **If your dog is stressed**, take him away from the exciting or frustrating situation to help calm him down.

In the long term:

While it should retract naturally, a dog's penis can sometimes get stuck outside of the "prepuce," or external furry skin that sheathes it. This can lead to dryness or tissue infection. Even worse, if the penis sticks out for just a few hours and blood supply is restricted, the tissue may suffer necrosis and need amputation. Check whether your dog's penis is still out after 10 minutes, because then he may need veterinary attention.

Dilated pupils
show arousal

Panting may indicate
a stress-based reaction

the function?

As well as for procreation, a red rocket is used by dogs to show they are feeling nonsexual arousal due to something worrying or exciting.

Dandruff and hair loss with a red rocket suggests anxiety

CENSORED

My dog growls at me

I've got a rescue dog and we get along really well, except sometimes she growls at me and my friends. Should I send her back? I don't want an aggressive dog.

What's my dog thinking?

Easy now. Your dog has probably had a difficult past and needs your help. The good news is she's giving you a clear warning that something isn't right. Dogs use an escalating sequence of behaviors to show they are uncomfortable (see pages 150–151). Like a gunslinger with a hand over their holster, a dog may growl while waiting to see if you will "draw" first or step back and make peace. Growling could also be caused by illness (see pages 136–137). Get professional help to assess the situation before you make any life-changing decisions.

"Airplane" ears pointing sideways signal a stand-off

Hard eyes: "I'm not messing!"

Scrunched muzzle draws lips back

Lip curls to offer a gun show

Low "fear growl" posture to look less threatening

the function?

Regardless of the reason—fear, frustration, or an attempt to intimidate—a growling dog is saying, "I don't want to bite you!"

> **66**
>
> Growling is good! A growling dog is not a biting dog. A growling dog is asking for help.
>
> **99**

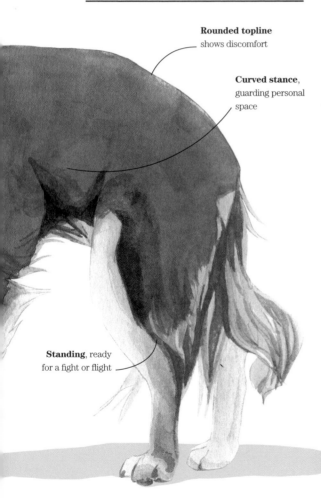

Rounded topline
shows discomfort

Curved stance, guarding personal space

Standing, ready for a fight or flight

What should I do?

In the moment:

- **Stand still and straight**, turned slightly to the side, so you are nonthreatening. Avoid staring at your dog and breathe evenly.
- **Your dog is uncomfortable**. Help her relax by giving her some space.
- **Don't scold your dog** for growling. If you punish her, it's more likely you'll get no warning next time and the dog will jump straight to biting.

In the long term:

- **Book a vet check-up** to see if your dog has a health problem.
- **Watch for any signs** of discomfort your dog shows before growling. When you notice these signs again, give her some space before she escalates to "swearing" at you.
- **A qualified behaviorist** can help you work out why your dog might be growling and find a loving way to change her behavior—or yours!

Warning or playtime

Dogs make a variety of amazing noises to communicate with us (see pages 12–13). They'll use growls to get attention or treats and even to start play. A play growl is often exaggerated and loud and may go from a high "chatty" tone to a low grumble and back again. In contrast, warning growls usually stay low and guttural.

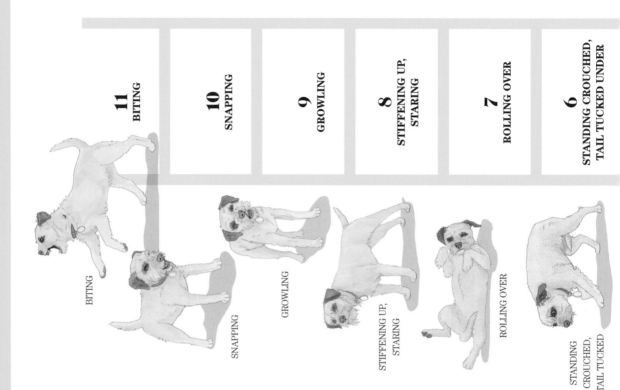

11 BITING	
10 SNAPPING	
9 GROWLING	
8 STIFFENING UP, STARING	
7 ROLLING OVER	
6 STANDING CROUCHED, TAIL TUCKED UNDER	

BITING

SNAPPING

GROWLING

STIFFENING UP, STARING

ROLLING OVER

STANDING CROUCHED, TAIL TUCKED

ADVANCED DOGWATCHING

Ladder of aggression

For dogs, repeated aggression can be fatal. So rather than fighting over the slightest drama, they have evolved a sequence of behaviors to help them avoid using their teeth unless it's absolutely necessary.

This "ladder" of escalating behaviors was conceptualized by veterinary behaviorist Dr. Kendal Shepherd to help us understand how dogs react if they feel stressed or threatened. All dogs start at the bottom with mild calming signals to appease, like a nose lick or yawn. If that signal is ignored or doesn't get the other dog or person to stop or back off, the dog will move up the ladder. Over time, dogs may learn not to bother with steps that haven't worked for them before and go straight to the "rung" that did, which

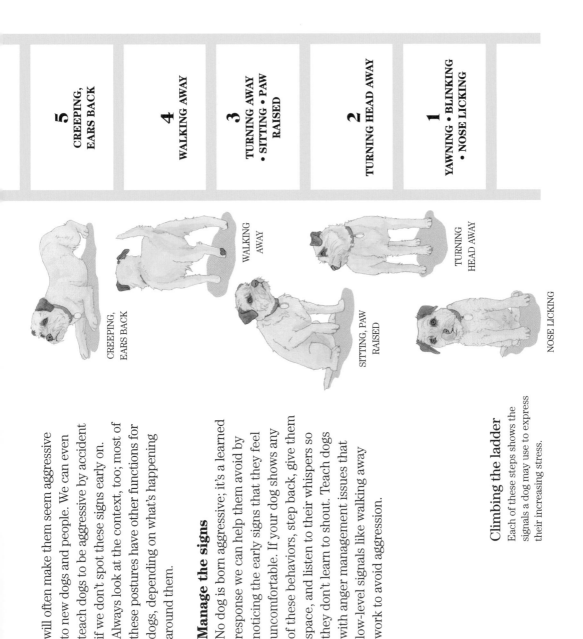

5 CREEPING, EARS BACK

4 WALKING AWAY

3 TURNING AWAY • SITTING • PAW RAISED

2 TURNING HEAD AWAY

1 YAWNING • BLINKING • NOSE LICKING

CREEPING, EARS BACK

WALKING AWAY

SITTING, PAW RAISED

TURNING HEAD AWAY

NOSE LICKING

will often make them seem aggressive to new dogs and people. We can even teach dogs to be aggressive by accident if we don't spot these signs early on. Always look at the context, too; most of these postures have other functions for dogs, depending on what's happening around them.

Manage the signs

No dog is born aggressive; it's a learned response we can help them avoid by noticing the early signs that they feel uncomfortable. If your dog shows any of these behaviors, step back, give them space, and listen to their whispers so they don't learn to shout. Teach dogs with anger management issues that low-level signals like walking away work to avoid aggression.

Climbing the ladder

Each of these steps shows the signals a dog may use to express their increasing stress.

My dog mouths and nips

Sometimes my dog mouths and even nips me. I know he's still a puppy and they're only gentle bites, but I don't want him to be a biter, and shouting at him makes it worse.

What's my dog thinking?

Don't stress; this is completely normal! Pups lose their baby teeth at around 5–6 months and naturally mouth or nip to relieve the pain of teething. And if your pup is excited, stressed, or doesn't want a fuss right now, mouthing or nipping your hand is the easiest way for him to tell you. Puppies also pick up, taste, chew, and test the world around them—their mouth is their "hands." While this oral obsession is used to train some fantastic assistance dogs, it can become habitual, so puppies need to learn early on that teeth on skin is never okay.

> **66**
>
> Biting is a breed-specific behavior for many dogs, including Terriers, Guarding, and Herding breeds, but it can be curbed with training.
>
> **99**

What should I do?

In the moment:

- **If you're playing** with your pup and you feel teeth, say "Ouch!" and pause play. If your dog comes back with another bite, give him a 10-second time-out in another room to show him that's not okay. If you're petting him when it happens, he's saying stop—so hands off, and use force-free handling.
- **Offer a frozen carrot** or a rubber toy. If your pup is teething, having something in his mouth will help soothe aching jaws.

In the long term:

- **Redirect gentle bites** onto toys, praising your dog for "good" bites on them. Then you can progress from training him not to nip to not mouthing altogether.
- **Make sure** your dog gets regular play breaks and naps. Puppies also mouth when they're overtired.
- **Monitor your pup's playmates**— both dog and human—as rough players will teach him bad habits, like biting to start a game.

Shark mouth

Nature provides puppies with tiny razor-sharp teeth to inflict maximum pain with minimum effort. Nipping tells the mom when to wean them off milk and onto solid foods. It also means pups get pushback from littermates and human family when they bite too hard. This teaches them to "inhibit" or soften their bite before they develop strong jaw muscles and adult teeth.

Playful posture:
"Don't get angry with me"

Nipping soothes
young jaws

Looking at you says,
"Talk to me!"

the function?

Testing surfaces, teething, attention-seeking, stress, and excitement are all common causes of gentle bites. What's your dog's "reward" for nipping?

My dog bites ... for real!

My dog has bitten me, my vet, and a couple of my friends.
I've managed to grab her and stop her a few other times,
but I never know when she might try again.

What's my dog thinking?

Most likely, that she has no other choice. We often assume—wrongly—that biting is always about aggression and intimidation. Fundamentally, though, your dog bites because she's learned that it works—either to get something, like attention, or get rid of someone, like a frightening person. Most dogs don't want to deliver bites, even when they're scared, because they could get injured, too; they'll only do it after trying less aggressive behaviors that don't achieve what they want (see pages 150–151). Any biting can have serious consequences for you and your dog. Fortunately, biting dogs can be fully rehabilitated with patience, positivity, and professional help.

What should I do?

In the moment:
- **Isolate your dog** and deal with the injury first. If skin is broken, the bite wound should be cleaned and medical attention, including an antibiotic injection, should be sought immediately.

- **Keep calm.** Punishing with pain or fear will make a dog more insecure and more likely to bite again.

In the long term:
- **Sudden aggressive behavior** may be a sign your dog is in pain, so book a vet checkup.
- **Call in a behaviorist** who uses force-free techniques and positive reinforcement training to teach your dog that biting isn't necessary to get others to go away or give her attention.
- **Manage the risk** by avoiding dogs, people, or situations you know could lead to your dog biting, and muzzle her for walks if she has bitten before.

> **"**
>
> The law is rarely on the dog's side, and even scaring someone could lead to a dog being put to sleep–so get professional support urgently!
>
> **"**

the function?

Biting isn't "bad"; it's purely functional. You need to work out whether it's driven by fear, frustration, over-confidence, or practice (see pages 22–23).

Facial and body tension, pumped with adrenaline

Ears slightly back in personal defense mode

Eyes stare directly at the "target"

Hard eyes and dilated pupils create a ferocious expression

Teeth clearly displayed and warning, "I don't want to bite!"

Forward, frozen posture, ready to bite and fight

Bite scale

This scale ranks the seriousness of biting, which is helpful when recording the details for your behaviorist:

1. **Air snap** is a warning, with no contact.
2. **Bite, release** is a single bite to discipline, test, or intimidate.
3. **Bite, bite, release** is a rally of bites, followed by a retreat.
4. **Bite, hold** is a confident bite to pin or subdue.
5. **Bite, hold, shake** is intended to kill.

SURVIVAL GUIDE

Introduce a new dog

We all love company, right? Wrong! Dogs are a social species, but getting another dog can easily make your first dog feel like they've got competition—unless you help them build a solid friendship.

1
Host playdates
Introduce a rescue dog before rehoming by taking it on lots of short walks with your first dog. Start by lead walking the dogs a few feet (meters) apart before you eventually let them off in a secure green space to meet.

2
Watch their play signals
Are they really getting along? If your new dog and your first dog start "playing" together for hours without any breaks, they are more than likely practicing for outright warfare! Help them take breaks using recall and mat-based relaxation training so they can settle, or redirect their play onto toys. Knowing the signs of fair play will help you referee with love (see pages 120–121).

3
Be the parent
Adult dogs can be patient with puppies to a point, but they need you to accept ultimate parenthood. If you're bringing a new puppy home, make sure your first dog has space to retreat and recharge.

4
Train them together
Teaching both dogs that you have enough time, attention, and treats for each of them is so important. Train them alongside each other so they learn that time spent together is delicious fun!

5
Separate their stuff
Each dog needs their own "bedroom" (a separate bed) and food dish to feel at home. Although they may choose to sleep together eventually, dogs never enjoy eating head to head.

My dog chases his tail

Every time we go to let the dog out into the yard, he chases his tail—it's so funny! Although it's a bit strange when he manages to catch it, then starts nibbling ...

the function?

All obsessive-compulsive behaviors, like tail chasing, are designed to soothe the dog in the short term by producing the feel-good hormone dopamine.

What's my dog thinking?

Chasing is instinctive for dogs and can be highly satisfying, but tail chasing is a sign of real distress. It often starts due to a motivational conflict, like wanting to pee outside but also being worried about a neighbor's dog. The dog's frustrated brain wants to go in different directions at the same time, which sends him turning in circles—like we'd pace up and down. Chasing tails, lights, shadows, cars, balls, and also overgrooming can become forms of obsessive-compulsive disorder. These unhelpful coping strategies can be damaging to dogs' health and need to be addressed. Some dogs also learn to use tail chasing to earn attention.

Bunched fur and dandruff are signs of stress

> **66**
>
> It's natural to laugh at things we don't understand. But repetitively chasing his tail, lights, or shadows isn't funny—or fun for your dog.
>
> **99**

What should I do?

In the moment:

- **Try not to laugh** at, reward, or encourage your dog to chase his tail for attention.
- **Calmly redirect** your dog's attention onto a game, food-based activity, or some training.

In the long term:

- **Consult a qualified behaviorist** who uses force-free techniques to help you analyze and manage your dog's anxiety. Note the situations, sounds, times, or environments that may trigger obsessive behavior.
- **Feeding 2–3 meals daily** will help regulate your dog's energy and sleep, and adequate mental and physical exercise will help him access natural relaxation.
- **If you crate your dog** for long periods while you're out, consider leaving the door open and getting someone to visit halfway through the day. Leaving "enrichment" activities like puzzle games and interactive feeders around your home will keep his mind focused.

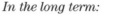

Ears back
in anxiety or frustration

Facial tension
says, "I'm not okay"

Chasing leads to chewing … a dangerous habit

Good frustration

The amount of stress adult dogs can cope with is determined at a young age, during periods of natural frustration, or "stress immunization." These shape the "neuroplasticity" of the pup's brain— its ability to adapt and rewire itself to form new coping strategies in response to new and changing environments and experiences. This is why weaning, playing with littermates, and short separations can all help strengthen a dog's resilience in later life.

My dog won't calm down

My dog gets frantic. At home and outdoors, she'll often go absolutely bonkers and just won't listen. She's even head-butted me, so I'm worried she could knock someone's tooth out!

What's my dog thinking?

This crazed playfulness tells us a dog is really *not* happy and needs our help to feel grounded again. When your dog is already stressed or excited—if someone new visits, or you're playing at the park—then looming over her, cuddling her, offering treats, or high-pitched greetings or excited vocal cues can push her over the edge into acute stress. In this "over threshold" state, a dog becomes hyperactive and can't hear you. If you hold her and tell her to stop, that's when a head-butt or "muzzle punch" can happen as a self-defense move to gain some space.

The five "Fs"

When both dogs and humans are confronted with something exciting or alarming, they can choose fight, flight, freeze, faint, or flirt as a response. For dogs, expressing fear as "flirt" can look like overexcitement or playfulness— just as we use comedy to break tension. Dogs also show us they are wound up in other ways, like a crazy half-hour, chewing our stuff, and tail chasing (see pages 42–43, 94–95, and 158–159).

What should I do?

In the moment:
- **Take your dog away** from the situation (or out of the room) and wait quietly with her on a loose lead until she calms down.
- **If you're indoors**, take her back into the same room and ask her to "Sit," "Go to bed," or "Stay," using treats to reward her for behaving more calmly. If you're outdoors, continue your walk or game, again rewarding calm behavior.

In the long term:
- **Tell family and friends**. Once they understand it's important not to wind up your dog, you can use social situations for training. But don't rush it: introduce her to exciting and scary triggers—like a doorbell—one by one.
- **Dogs need a quiet place** to sleep and at least an hour of mental and physical stimulation daily—twice that for breeds like German Shepherds, Huskies, and Collies.
- **Dog food** that's protein rich and preservative free can help.

the function?

"Manic panic" is the dog trying to cope when too much adrenaline suddenly kicks in during a situation that's already exciting or scary.

Facial stress lines say, "I'm freaked out!"

Dilated pupils show she's pumped with adrenaline

"Spatulate" tongue, wider at the bottom, signals stress

Jumping up to release pent-up energy

Flushing skin shows through fur as blood races

My dog won't shut up

My dog is a real chatterbox. He whines, woofs, and squeaks at me all day long— whether I'm on the phone, watching TV, or even in the bathroom. It's driving me crazy!

the function?

Your dog could be asking for attention because he wants something, saying he's feeling playful or excited, or alerting you to danger, among other functions.

What's my dog thinking?

How cute is it when you ask your dog a question and get an enthusiastic "Arooo!" back? Guess what: when you reply, he is thinking you're a well-trained human who responds to *his* vocal cues! And once he knows it gets your attention, he'll keep on "talking." Whether you have a Siberian Husky that says hello, a squeaky Springer Spaniel, or even a Terrier that sings to Taylor Swift, unwanted vocalizing can soon start to feel like water torture. Some breeds are genetically vocal, and vocalizing has numerous functions (see page 13). But for most, the good news is that you trained this behavior, so you can untrain it, too.

> 66
>
> Domesticated dogs have evolved a huge repertoire of noises compared to wolves just to communicate with us–the little legends!
>
> 99

What should I do?

In the moment:

- **Don't tell** your dog to shut up. It doesn't work, and he'll believe you're joining in.
- **If you think** your dog is attention-seeking, don't give him what he wants. Barking to get you to look down, come back, fetch something, or feed him will keep happening if you reinforce it by complying.

In the long term:

- **Notice your dog's behavior** around dinner time, when you're playing, and when you open doors or crawl behind furniture to retrieve toys. Is he always using his voice to ask you for different things?
- **Get the whole family** to help train the dog to ask for things with alternative behaviors, like "touch" (with a paw) or by holding a toy. Make sure no one gives him what he wants for whining or barking.

Soft facial muscles
show vocalizing isn't due
to anxiety or threat

No quick fixes

Anti-bark products are all designed in
some way to punish dogs for barking
by spraying, shocking, or freaking them
out. Quick-fix solutions like this may
negatively affect dogs' mental and
physical well-being long term
and aren't changing the
underlying reason for the
behavior—for example,
if your dog barks
while you're out
(see pages
178–179).

No teeth showing
means no drama

SURVIVAL GUIDE

Fireworks season

When the bangs begin and the sky explodes in color, most dogs will run and hide. Fireworks season is tough, but there are things you can do to stop frightened dogs from shooting off like rockets.

1
Tire them out

Take your dog for a nice long walk during the daytime and do a brain-training session with them as well to help them feel sleepy and relaxed before any fireworks start.

2
Help them relax

A long-lasting chew or stuffed food toy is a wonderful distraction from loud bangs or weird noises. Using a pheromone-based collar or a plug-in diffuser can also help your dog find their zen.

3
Make a den

Create a covered safe space for your dog to retreat to, wherever they feel safest—even under your bed. Closing curtains and playing some music indoors will muffle the noise of fireworks, too.

4
Comfort, don't coddle

If you show your dog you are worried about them, they will only get worse. You can comfort a dog with affection and voice without joining them in their anxiety by cuddling, overstroking, or cooing, "Aww, poor baby! It's okay." Tell them you're fine by smiling and relaxing with them.

5
Prep your pup

Get puppies used to loud noises as early as possible. A "socialization soundtrack," with noises including fireworks and baby cries, can be paired with treats or an exciting toy to help your dog learn a buffet of joy arrives when strange noises happen. After all, trained Gundogs aren't worried by the sound of gunshot!

My dog won't fetch

I've given up playing fetch with my dog. Mostly, she runs off with the ball and rips it up. Other dogs love fetching things—why doesn't she?

What's my dog thinking?

Most dogs will chase something fast moving, but what happens next is down to a combination of the dog's breed and their previous experience of playing fetch. For example, Terriers are bred to kill vermin, so when you throw a squeaky ball, their instinct will be to shred it rather than return it to you. We can accidentally discourage our dogs from fetching by assuming they naturally want to share; if they don't, chasing them and fishing the ball or toy out of their mouth will only make your dog run away.

Teaching fetch:

- **Start with two of the same** toy or ball—keeping one in your pocket and one in your hand— so you have something to trade with your dog.
- **Show your dog the toy** and pretend she can't have it! Jog around with it until your dog follows you.
- **Throw or roll the toy** and praise your dog for chasing or biting it.
- **If your dog picks it up** immediately, move away. This encourages her to come closer to you with the toy in her mouth.
- **As your dog gets closer**, take out the second toy, turn toward her, lift the toy high, and say, "Drop!"
- **Always wait** for your dog to drop the first toy, *then* throw the second one. Be patient and be sure to keep the game friendly.

Tip: If your dog isn't toy motivated, use food-dispensing balls for a few weeks instead.

Five stages of fetch

Some breeds are naturally more likely to enjoy playing fetch than others, but overall, fetch is a five-stage game of trust that has to be taught. The dog must chase, bite, carry, walk toward you, and drop—it's pretty complicated. A problem with any one of these stages can cause your dog to duck out of playing entirely, so you may need to deconstruct and rebuild each stage of the game together.

High tail: aroused from the chase and alert to surroundings

Terriers are bred to kill, not carry!

> 66
>
> Disemboweling the "kill" comes after the hunt. If your dog is ball ripping, she may be saying she's finished with the game.
>
> 99

the function?

Often dogs keep the ball because you don't offer anything equal or better to trade for it, or they learn fun things happen when they play "keep away."

Standing to rip allows for quick escape from ambush

Chewing or ripping soothes after an exciting hunt

167

My dog won't come back

When I call my dog, he pretends not to hear and walks off. I trained him as a puppy and he knows it drives me crazy when he won't come straight back. What's his problem?

the function?

For your dog, avoiding you is a good way of getting a longer walk and not coming near while you're likely to tell him off.

Ambling gently away, reluctant to go home

Lowered head and tail, an appeasing posture

Mouth closed, cautious and tense

Sniffing as a calming signal, waiting for you to cheer up

What's my dog thinking?

Your dog would rather stay clear, just until you stop shouting or shaking his lead at him. While dogs, like children, learn at a young age to appease impatient people, later on they work out that sometimes it's best to avoid stressful situations until things calm down. There's also a good chance your dog knows when a walk is ending just by the tone of your voice—so he may not come back quickly, as then the fun is over! Getting angry won't help; it's time to rebuild your recall bond.

What should I do?

In the moment:

- **Breathe and smile**. This is a communication malfunction, not a challenge to your authority. Your dog responds to your face, so shake it off and cheer up!
- **Walk away** and stop calling your dog. Try changing direction and even running away to get your dog interested in what you're up to.

In the long term:

- **Go back to basics** and have fun! Practice recalling your dog from a few feet (meters) away at home and in the yard using high-value treats.
- **Attach a 32-foot** (10-meter) training lead to your dog for safety and retrain him using fear-free techniques. That way, if you call and

> " Scolding your dog for not coming back immediately when you call is a surefire way to ruin your recall relationship. "

he doesn't come back while you're at the park, you can still get to the lead and ensure he's under control.

Nose on, ears off

Often, if a dog's nose is "on" and they are lost in the world of smell, their ears are "off" and they genuinely can't hear you. Smell is a dog's primary sense and, like our eyes for us, their noses deliver the most vivid detail about the world (see pages 12–13). Dogs have all sorts of interesting "chats" via their noses with tufts of grass, trash, and lampposts.

My dog won't stop pulling

My dog always pulls ahead, comes back for a treat, then pulls again—she's almost dragged me into the road! I've tried every kind of collar, harness, and face gear, but she won't stop pulling.

What's my dog thinking?

From a dog's perspective, the lead is weird. They're off the lead for 98 percent of their life at home, then suddenly when we go somewhere, we get clingy and attach them to us—and they have no choice about where we take them. Pulling is *the* most common training and behavioral issue; prolific pullers spoil walks and often become reactive to other dogs and people as a result. Your dog doesn't want to get dragged around any more than you do—fortunately, the key to success is a mix of training, treats, and patience.

Panting due to stress or gasping for breath

Choke chains and slip leads create pain and fear-based learning

Tension on the collar makes the dog feel trapped

Opposition reflex

Dogs naturally pull away from us to keep their balance—it's called their "opposition reflex." This means you should be careful to keep the lead loose yourself, using treats to invite your dog to follow and work with you, not against you. Be aware: if your dog pulls behind you, there may be something scary ahead, so don't ruin your relationship by dragging her toward it.

Tension on the lead
is also caused by
holding it high

the function?

Dogs pull because they want to get somewhere or get away from something quickly, or because they've been trained to believe that's how the lead works.

Tense tail carriage:
aroused and frustrated

Legs tense and braced
in opposition reflex

What should I do?

Begin again to rebuild trust. Practice teaching your dog to walk by your side off lead at home, using treats to get her to follow you.

Reward walking with walking. Whenever your dog starts to pull, stop walking and wait until she comes back to your side. Then set off together again and treat her regularly for staying close to you.

Every step you take while your dog is pulling is a reward, so be consistent for a month, even if it means shorter walks.

Use other rewards as well as treats, like sniff spots or other dogs. Show your dog you'll get to these rewards together, on a loose lead.

Only walk your dog when you have time, so you aren't tempted to let her pull because you're rushing.

66

Yanking, scolding, and keeping the lead tight or short will all encourage your dog to pull—as being close to you isn't fun.

99

171

My dog hates his harness

My dog loves walks, so why does he run and hide when I get the harness out? Once I've finally put it on him, he stands there looking sad, like he's forgotten how to walk.

the function?

Cowering, running away, growling, or even becoming playful all show your dog is scared of your body language or what you're putting on him.

What's my dog thinking?

Dogs are loved, respected, and free to roam the house, yet when it's time for a walk, we suddenly capture them and shove their heads and feet into a restrictive harness or coat! This is a total invasion of personal space, so it's no surprise if dogs go into shut-down mode and cower or freeze at the weird feeling on their back. Teaching your dog to enjoy all walking equipment is crucial; for a reactive dog, it can be the difference between a calm or a stressful walk.

Training to get dressed

Let your dog progress at his own pace and escape when he wants. This training may take 3–4 sessions:

- **Put the harness** (or coat, muzzle, and so on) on the floor and scatter treats around it to encourage your dog to come over. Let him eat the treats, then pick up the harness and treat him again for approaching you.

- **Holding a treat**, put your hand through the head opening and let your dog take it; do this 10 times.
- **Bring your hand back** toward you, inviting your dog to put his head into the harness to eat. Take it off and walk away; again, repeat this step 10 times.
  Tip: Make it fun by jogging, so your dog chases you first.
- **Rest the harness** on your dog's back or rub the dog's shoulders and neck with it while he eats a treat.
- **Scatter treats** on the floor around the dog so your hands are free to secure the harness as he eats.

    "

Coats, harnesses, clothing, vet collars, and muzzles all require training to wear comfortably and confidently.

"

Why use a harness?

Harnessing protects a dog's neck, which is actually very delicate. The neck houses lymph nodes for fighting disease; saliva-producing glands; and the all-important thyroid, which produces hormones that help regulate the dog's fight, flight, and relaxation responses. Putting repeated pressure on the neck with choke collars, or yanking on a collar and lead, could damage important glands, fracture neck vertebrae, and collapse the windpipe.

Shut-down posture as a "survival" strategy

Turning away means "I don't want trouble"

Soft eyes, appeasing you

Tail tucked under to cover anal glands

Ears back, wanting to run away

Mouth closed and jaw clenched from tension

My dog hates people

I got my dog at 6 months, and she must have been badly treated, because she hates people. When guests come visit she growls, barks, or runs away and hides, even if they go to pet her.

What's my dog thinking?

It could be "Leave me alone," "I need space," "I don't like how they smell," or even "They're wearing something weird!" Whatever the variation, fundamentally your dog is telling you she doesn't feel safe and needs your help. Dogs can learn to fear people from their dog or human parents, a lack of human contact during their key development stage as puppies (8–16 weeks), or because someone spooked them during their natural "fear phase" (usually 17–20 weeks). Fearful avoidance can quickly switch to aggression. Even so, dogs are always learning, so you can help your pooch feel more people-positive, whatever their age.

66

While we want to show people we're managing an "unfriendly" dog, correcting your dog will teach her to shut down and fear you instead.

99

What should I do?

In the moment:

- **Calmly remove** your dog from the situation. Scolding her will only make her more nervous.
- **Pair the arrival** or sight of people with something your dog finds really tasty or rewarding to shift her underlying emotion from panic to positivity.

In the long term:

- **Watch closely** for early warning signs of distress. If you see them, let the dog escape rather than escalate toward aggressive behavior like growling (see pages 150–151).
- **Don't answer the door together**, especially holding your dog's collar—associating rough handling with people arriving will make her more fearful. If necessary, put her in another room before inviting guests in (see pages 96–97).
- **Ask people** not to stare at or try to pet your dog. In public, muzzling is a good way to discourage any unwanted petting.

Identify triggers

It's easy to mislabel our dogs' unusual behavior. A dog that snaps at someone who stops to say hello may not be a "people hater"; this reaction could actually be caused by a sequence of events. The dog may be able to cope with three people petting them, but a fourth is one too many triggers, causing them to snap—literally! (See pages 24–25 and 26–27.)

"Airplane" ears guard space to stop the person from coming close

Eyes assessing danger

the function?

This is usually fear-induced escape, avoidance, or aggression. Notice what happens before and after to work out why the dog is fearful (see pages 22-23).

Lowered, crouching posture says, "Don't look at me"

Using furniture or "self-cornering" to protect herself from ambush

SURVIVAL GUIDE

In the car

Whether you're running to the pet store or heading out onto the open road for an adventure, it's essential to keep your pooch safe and train them to feel comfortable in the car.

1
Socialize first

Slowly introduce your dog to the sight, smell, sound, and movement of the car for a few minutes at a time initially, then extend the time period. Keep journeys short at first, with lots of treats on hand as a reward. Puppy inner ears are still developing, so they will experience motion sickness more vividly, and bad beginners driving lessons are hard to forget!

2
Crate for safety

Dogs must be secured for travel, ideally in a crate, to stop them from being a distraction to you or a danger to themselves and everyone else if you're involved in an accident. Train your dog using treats to get in and out of the crate at home, in the yard, and then finally in the car, using ramps if necessary.

3
Soothe car sickness

Let dogs that get car sick see out of a window to get some perspective, and open one to distract them with fresh air smells. Lavender and chamomile smells can soothe, too. Offer charcoal biscuits for sickness, and don't tell your dog off if they vomit or potty in the car, as this is often stress related.

4
Pick a pawfect destination!

Get your dog to associate the car with fun; only using it to go to the vets or to drop them at a kennels is the quickest way to create car phobia. Plan long journeys beforehand to include lots of breaks during the trip and a positive destination, like the beach, a nature walk, or the pet store.

My dog hates being left

It breaks my heart to leave my dog every day. He howls and scratches the door, and I always come home to a dirty protest— but I've got to go to work.

Howling deep distress, a sound designed to call from far away

Body tension and discomfort

Tail low and body cowering

Stress urination, a sign of adrenaline and fear

What's my dog thinking?

"When will I see you again?" is what a dog with separation anxiety "sings" when that front door closes. Dogs are social creatures and they need you to survive, so naturally your dog has a small panic attack when left to fend for himself at home. He may bark, howl, pee, and scratch or chew a barrier like a door or anything nearby. This isn't "bad" behavior; it's a cry for help! It takes perseverance, but you can reduce separation anxiety, especially with the help of a qualified, compassionate dog behaviorist.

What should I do?

Build up separation gradually, especially with puppies and rescue dogs; it can take 2 months of training before you can leave them for 3–5 hours.

Create a separation routine. First, encourage your dog to relax on a mat, apart from you. Then progress to putting him in his "bedroom" after walks; use a baby gate or pen and leave him with a food-stuffed toy for 10 minutes. Aim to increase this by 5 minutes per day.

You must be around, in another room, so you can listen and return to praise your dog for good choices like being quiet, lying down, or playing

> Getting another dog won't stop your hound from feeling lonely. Once a dog has bonded to you, they will still struggle to see you go.

with a toy. Learning what he needs to do to get you to reappear will help soothe his anxiety.

When your dog is eventually settled enough to leave alone, it helps if he's fed, exercised, and has a high-value reward. Dogs relax best in the room where they sleep; don't use a crate, unless he already does by choice.

Be calm and go. Emotional goodbyes and greetings upset dogs even more.

Frustration or panic?

It's normal for dogs to feel frustrated while learning a separation routine; separation anxiety is part "barrier frustration" and part fear of being abandoned. A frustrated dog can still learn, so don't go back to them if they're whining. But a dog in panic mode is too lost in emotion to understand anything and needs you to return. Dogs vocalize their feelings during training; listen and respond to this (pages 12–13).

My dog hates being bathed or groomed

My dog will happily leap into a puddle or a river, but she hates me bathing her, and at the salon, she flips out and tries to bite the groomer.

What's my dog thinking?

"Bathtime!" strikes fear into the bravest pets, and your dog has every reason to hate the grooming salon, too. From her perspective, it's a chamber of horrors; one minute she's relaxing on the couch at home, and the next she's noosed to a table and surrounded by clippers, snippers, dryers, pliers, coat-tugging brushes, cages, water hoses, and stinky, people-pleasing shampoos! Grooming is a social activity for dogs and should be as gentle and relaxing as possible. It can be a fun experience for both you and your dog, if you retrain her to love the groomer.

Hard eyes say, "I'm serious!"

Ears back in the direction of retreat

Showing teeth, a warning the dog could bite

Sideways posture: "I'll walk away when you walk away"

Tail down or sitting to cover the anal glands

Designer coat disaster

Cockapoos are a popular "designer" crossbreed, but their fur is a man-made grooming nightmare. The combination of sleek Cocker Spaniel hair and watertight Poodle curls creates a coat that matts against the skin in a matter of days without regular grooming. Cockapoos require lots of daily brushing right down to the base of the coat to stop them from getting tied up in knots.

What should I do?

In the moment:

If your pooch freaks out at the groomers, take her home and let her calm down. Forcing your dog to accept rushed grooming, or punishing her for showing aggression, will ruin your bond and teach your dog to be even more defensive more quickly next time. At home, stop grooming if you see any early signs of discomfort or stress (see pages 150–151) and only begin again when your dog is willing to participate.

the function?

A dog that moves away, lunges, or nips a groomer has been trained by previous insensitive handling or is uncomfortable due to a matted coat (see pp. 150–151).

In the long term:

- **Patiently desensitize** your dog to each bathing and grooming sensation one by one, using multiple sessions, treats, and play breaks to reduce her underlying fear.
- **A dog behaviorist** can help take the process back to basics, touching and treating your dog while handling the "subliminal bite trigger zones" (ears, neck, bottom, and feet) before introducing grooming equipment.
- **A licking mat** or food-based toy gives your dog something fun to do during grooming and leaves your hands free to work.

SURVIVAL GUIDE

Vets and groomers

Dogs are easy to train. So let's train them to understand what's expected of them at the vet's and groomer's and relieve the stress, instead of rushing them in and getting them "done" quickly.

1

Practice runs

Take your dog to visit the vet and groomer several times to earn treats and to build a bond with the person before they have to trust them when they are sick or in need of a haircut.

2

Handle with care

Practice handling daily, using treats to show your dog that having parts of their body touched is fun! Watch their body language for stress signs, and show them you'll stop when they need a break.

3

The right groomer

Look for a groomer who doesn't use force or restraints and who will take time to work gently with your dog. Professionals who rush dogs can teach them to become nervous or aggressive.

4

Muzzle up!

You can teach a dog to enjoy putting their head into a muzzle as a fun training exercise at home (see pages 172–173). Some vets insist on muzzling dogs for uncomfortable procedures, and you will make this much less traumatic for your dog by helping them prepare for this scenario way in advance.

5

Distract with tricks

Teach your dog tricks like "touch" (with their nose), "chin" (resting their chin against your hand or a surface), or "flat dog" (lying down) and invite them to offer bits of their body as part of your daily training. Getting your dog to focus on a trick is a great way to distract them when a strange stethoscope or nail clippers appear.

Index

Breed index

Resources

Further reading

Dogs Desmond Morris

How Dogs Learn Mary R. Burch, Jon S. Bailey

In Defence of Dogs John Bradshaw

Behavior Adjustment Training 2.0 Grisha Stewart

Interactive Play Guide Craig Ogilvie

Inside of a Dog: What Dogs See, Smell, and Know Alexandra Horowitz

Being a Dog: Following the Dog into a World of Smell Alexandra Horowitz

The Truth About Wolves and Dogs Toni Shelbourne

Canine Body Language Brenda Aloff

Lucy's Law: The Story of a Little Dog Who Changed the World Marc Abraham

Online

www.pawfectdogsense.com

www.amplifiedbehaviour.com Online video advice library

www.naturallyhappydogs.com Dog behavior, positive reinforcement-based training, and health advice

www.fearfreepets.com Advice on fear-free handling of pets

www.psychologytoday.com/gb/blog/canine-corner Award-winning blog and articles

www.whole-dog-journal.com Natural dog care, behavior, and training

Kikopup YouTube training and behavior channel

www.battersea.org.uk/pet-advice/dog-advice Behavior, training, and health advice

www.bluecross.org.uk Behavior, training, and health advice

Find a dog behaviorist

Author's note: It's vital to find a specialist dog behaviorist who is fully qualified, uses force-free techniques and positive training methods, and has extensive professional experience. The industry is not yet regulated in the US (although various organizations claim to be the ultimate national or international register), and while vets are often asked for a recommendation, many are unsure about how to measure the quality of behaviorists. A "qualified" behaviorist should have a degree-level or higher qualification in animal or canine behavior and at least 1 year's practical experience with more than 100 dogs (or several years' direct practice under a behaviorist with such a qualification), plus a detailed understanding of learning theory principles in psychology. Dogs learn through conditioning, and a qualified behaviorist will offer solutions involving positive reinforcement, desensitization, and counter-conditioning and favor pain-free and fear-free training techniques. Anyone who tries to "fix" a problem like aggression in one session, "corrects" the dog with painful equipment before looking at the behavior's reinforcement history, or practices out-of-date "top dog" theory, does not have enough education in dog psychology and will damage your dog's ability to learn. Dogs do not learn by following "strong" leaders; don't be intimidated by confidence or maverick approaches or pay for training you don't feel entirely comfortable with. Always ask to see how the trainer or behaviorist handles a dog before giving them yours to work with. Does the dog they're handling look relaxed, happy, or confident? While they may seem "obedient," harsh handling leads dogs to become shut down and fearful and has no place in dog behavior management.

References

12 Communicating with scent

A. Horowitz, **Inside of a Dog: What Dogs See, Smell, and Know**, Simon & Schuster UK, 2012, p.72.

38 My dog can tell time

A. Horowitz, **Being a Dog: Following the Dog Into a World of Smell**, Simon & Schuster UK, 2016, pp.22–23.

58 My dog likes eating grass

K. L. C. Sueda, B. L. Hart, and K. D. Cliff, "Characterization of plant eating in dogs," **Applied Animal Behavior Science** 111, no. 2 (2008), pp.120–132.
DOI: https://doi.org/10.1016/j.aplanim.2007.05.018

72 My dog melts me with a look

J. Kaminski, B. M. Waller, R. Diogo, A. Hartstone-Rose, and A. M. Burrows, "Evolution of facial muscle anatomy in dogs," **Proceedings of the National Academy of Sciences of the USA (PNAS)** 116, no. 29 (2019), pp.14677–14681.
DOI: www.pnas.org/content/116/29/14677

136 Signs of illness

V. Bécuwe-Bonnet, M. C. Bélanger, D. Frank, J. Parent, and P. Hélie, "Gastrointestinal disorders in dogs with excessive licking of surfaces," **Journal of Veterinary Behavior** 7, no. 4 (2012), pp.194–204.
DOI: https://doi.org/10.1016/j.jveb.2011.07.003

Acknowledgments

Author's acknowledgments

Writing this book has been a joy and a journey. I would like to thank the late Dr. Sophia Yin for inspiring me to spread passionate and compassionate animal education. Thank you, Temple Grandin, for proving to a teenage Hannah that looking at the world differently means you're better equipped to change it. Thank you, Medical Detection Dogs, for proving that dogs can smell cancer and changing the course of my whole life. Thank you to my incredible parents for always telling me I can do whatever I set my mind to and for loving and helping me navigate every mountain and valley. Thank you, Dogs Trust, for sending me on training courses, challenging my thinking, and helping me set my sights on prevention rather than cure. Thank you to those that said I couldn't. Thank you, DK, Red Sky Productions, and Channel 4, for knowing that I can and making sure I have. Thank you to my editors Alastair and Andrea and art editor Alison for your patience, skill, and positivity. Thank you, Birmingham City Council, for letting me train dogs in public parks for 10 years. Thank you to every single one of my clients for your trust, your support, and your encouragement. Thank you, Chloe, my friend, for being the single most consistent cheerleader a witless sole training twentysomething could ever have. Thank you, Max the Wheaten Terrier, for being the ultimate dog wingman and my Yoda. Thank you, Falkor, my dog, for teaching me humility and humanity. Thank you to all of the team at Pawfect Dogsense, past and present; you all thrive on improving the future of dog welfare. Thank you, God, for giving me such a clear calling and a job I get deep joy from daily. And thank you to all the dogs for being the most patient, understanding, and forgiving teachers that I, and anyone reading this book, will ever hope to know.

Publisher's acknowledgments

DK would like to thank Marie Lorimer for indexing and Anne Newman for proofreading.

About the author

Hannah Molloy is a behavior specialist and managing director of two education companies: Pawfect Dogsense CIC and Amplified Behaviour. Her businesses provide bespoke behavior management plans and education courses for animal owners, rescues, vets, and pet stores, using positive reinforcement training techniques and fear-free handling.

Hannah has studied and worked with dogs for more than 15 years and is a "bond over obedience" trainer. Having earned a BSc Honors Degree in Animal Behavior (with her dissertation published in *Applied Animal Behaviour Science*, the official journal of the International Society for Applied Ethology), she worked in animal rescues and zoos, and as training and behavioral adviser for Dogs Trust, the UK's leading dog welfare charity. Her areas of special interest are dog body language, cultural attitudes to dog ownership, and the human–canine bond.

Hannah has regularly been a guest on BBC Radio and also features as an expert behaviorist on *Puppy School*, a Channel 4 television series helping new owners learn how to raise happy, well-socialized dogs.

She has a passion for improving animal welfare by teaching humans about animal communication and has designed numerous educational programs, providing training in colleges, pet stores, rescue centers, and veterinary practices. Her current educational work includes consulting on an NHS dog bite-prevention scheme to reduce bites on children and launching The Dog Education Project, with the long-term goal of providing free dog training classes and behavioral support for dog owners with low incomes.

In her spare time, Hannah enjoys scent training and dog parkour with her dog, Falkor.

About the illustrator

Mark Scheibmayr is an illustrator specializing in pet portraiture, based in Toronto, Canada. With ample time spent drawing dogs, and as a proud co-parent to a rescue dog, he is well practiced in both observing and illustrating canine communication. Mark is a regular contributor to the lifestyle website DobbernationLOVES and provides editorial illustrations for DK and Chapters Indigo. Other illustration work includes campaigns for the Town of Milton and exhibition materials for the Markham Museum, in his role as its exhibition designer. See more of his work at **markscheibmayr.com**.

Image credits